BROKEN

TIMELINES

Book 2: Mesopotamia

JACK STORNOWAY

Copyright

While every precaution has been taken in the preparation of this book, the publisher assumes no responsibility for errors or omissions, or for damages resulting from the use of the information contained herein.

BROKEN TIMELINES - BOOK 2: MESOPOTAMIA

First edition. December 27, 2019

Copyright © 2019 Jack Stornoway

ISBN: 978-1990289934

Table of Contents

TABLE OF CONTENTS

TABLE OF CONTENTS

Introduction

The timelines of Mesopotamia and Egypt are the two pillars that ancient history is built around, unfortunately, as the Egyptian timeline was more developed by the early-1900s it has traditionally taken precedence over the Mesopotamian timeline. This means whenever the Egyptian timeline is changed by Egyptologists, the Mesopotamian timeline needs to be adjusted by Assyriologists to keep the two timelines in sync. Unlike Egypt, where one civilization rose and fell repeatedly for thousands of years, in Mesopotamia various civilizations rose and fell. The oldest known culture in the region was the Sumerian culture, which was ultimately supplanted by the Akkadian civilization. The Akkadian civilization then devolved into the Babylonian and Assyrian cultures.

When the academic study of ancient Mesopotamian cultures began in the 1600s, Assyria was the oldest known Mesopotamian civilization, and as a result, the field of study is still known as Assyriology. Through the 1700s and 1800s, early excavations in Iraq uncovered the ruins of Babylon, and evidence of the Akkadian language, and by the 1850s evidence of the Sumerian language, although it was not translated until the early 1900s. The Sumerian civilization was established in history books by the 1910s, followed by the earlier Jamdet Nasr, Uruk, and Ubaid periods in 1930.

The records that have survived from the Sumerian and Akkadian periods list a series of ancient dynasties going back tens of thousands of years, which might have been considered history if Egypt did not exist. Unfortunately for Assyriologists, Egypt does exist. The similarities between the early dynastic periods of both cultures were documented by 1900, which essentially proved that one culture influenced the other. The question was which culture influenced the other? Both Egyptian hieroglyphs and Akkadian cuneiform had been translated by the late-1800s, and both have the same unique logographic, syllabic and alphabetic elements, which indicate that both derive from a common ancestor, and the question again was which one? Likewise, both cultures built flat-topped buildings in the early period, and then started building pyramidal structures, again, which culture influenced which? The common elements go far beyond writing forms and structural design, the two cultures even shares mythical animals, such as the serpopard.

On the next page is a photograph of the Narmer Palette from pre-Dynastic Egypt, and on the following page is a photograph of an Uruk Period seal from Mesopotamia, each featuring serpopards. In the early 1900s the question of which culture influenced which was easily answered, as the Sumerian cuneiform evolved from a pictographic script, similar to primitive hieroglyphs, the Sumerian form must have been based on the Egyptian form. As most Egyptologists were still using the long timeline, in which the 1st Egyptian Dynasty was founded in 5510 BC, it made sense that a pictographic script could be in use in Mesopotamia during the late pre-Dynastic period. Unfortunately, Egyptologists then decided to switch to the short timeline, and by the 1950s the 1st Egyptian Dynasty wasn't founded until 3100 BC, by which time the Sumerians had already invented cuneiform. This means that now Egyptian hieroglyphs were based on the Sumerian pictographs, even though they were no longer in use when hieroglyphs were invented.

Assyriologists were forced to change the accepted timeline of Mesopotamia to keep it in sync with the new short-timeline being used by Egyptologists, which created many anachronisms, including the Standard of Ur, pictured on the next page, showing horses and war-chariots in use in Sumer as early as 2600 BC, while they would not be introduced to Egypt until circa 1674 BC. The idea that the Egyptians traded with the Sumerians and Akkadians for almost 1000 years without bothering to import horses or core technologies like the chariot, or even the wheel, is simply impossible. The Sumerians would have conquered the Egyptians if they fell behind 1000 years in technology.

These compressed timelines, referred to herein as the Conventional Mesopotamian Timeline (CMT), and the Conventional Egyptian Timeline (CET), create far more anachronisms during the so-called dark-ages of Egyptian and Mesopotamian history, as there are few records to go on. One of these anachronisms is the Hyksos invasion of Egypt in the CET, which according to the CMT, simply did not happen. That the Hyksos entered Egypt from Canaan after conquering Byblos cannot be denied, yet, according to the Mesopotamian records from the time, they were not there, however, there was an identical people a couple of centuries later called the Mitannians.

The compression of the Egyptian and Mesopotamian timelines fans out to all cultures that traded with either the Egyptians or the Mesopotamians, erasing large sections of Indian, Greek, and Armenian history. The Broken Timelines series attempts to create an alternative framework, one based on the original long timeline of Egyptian and Sumerian history, which is what our ancient ancestors actually recorded. By restoring the original Egyptian timeline, the Mesopotamian timeline is permitted to decompress, and the anachronisms disappear. This long timeline is referred to as the Universal Long Timeline (ULT), as it attempts to unify all the ancient histories.

Part 1: Dynastic Mesopotamia

MESOPOTAMIAN ARCHAEOLOGICAL TIMELINE		
PERIOD	**CMT**	**ULT**
Ubaid 0	6500 to 5400 BC	8331 to 7231 BC
Ubaid 1	5400 to 4800 BC	7231 to 6631 BC
Ubaid 3	4800 to 4500 BC	6631 to 6331 BC
Late Ubaid	4500 to 4000 BC	6331 to 5831 BC
Early Uruk	4000 to 3800 BC	5831 to 5631 BC
Middle Uruk	3800 to 3400 BC	5831 to 5631 BC
Late Uruk	3400 to 3100 BC	5631 to 5231 BC
Jemdet Nasr	3100 to 2900 BC	4931 to 4731 BC
SITES	**CARBON DATED TIMELINE**	
Natufian	13,050 to 7505 BC	
Qaramel	13,000 to 6783 BC	
Jericho	9500 to 1400 BC	
Göbekli Tepe	9130 to 7370 BC	
Byblos	8800 BC until the present	
Aswad	8700 to 7500 BC	
Nevalı Çori	8400 to 8100 BC	
Hassuna	7750 to 6780 BC	
Çatalhöyük	7500 to 5700 BC	

The Conventional Mesopotamian Timeline is largely based on correlations with James Henry Breasted's short timeline of Dynastic Egyptian history, which was designed to make Egyptian history fit into the Biblical Timeline. Breasted funded expeditions to Iraq in the 1920s through his position at the Oriental Institute, which among other things cemented his para-biblical timeline within Assyriology. This timeline was originally considered proven by the layer of alluvium found in the ruins of southern Iraq that were seen as proof of the biblical global flood. This layer of alluvium ultimately proved to be from many river floods, which happened over several thousand years through the Ubaid-era. As a result, the original Ubaid, Uruk, and Jemdet Nasr periods have been extended back from 4000 to 2900 BC, to 6500 to 2900 BC.

This extended Conventional Mesopotamian Timeline is based on the comparison of different levels of cultural development at the times of the floods, and not a carbon-dated timeline. While this timeline does allow the Mesopotamian civilization to have developed over several thousand years, instead of suddenly appearing around 4000 BC, it still leaves the Mesopotamian civilization springing up around 6500 BC, after most of the carbon-dated ruins in the Middle East had been abandoned. The Natufian ruins in the Levant have been carbon-dated to between 13,050 to 7505 BC. The ruins of Qaramel in Syria have been carbon-dated to 13,000 to 6783 BC. The ruins of Göbekli Tepe in southeast Turkey have been carbon-dated to between 9130 and 7370 BC. The ruins of Tell Aswad in Syria have been carbon-dated to between 8700 and 7500 BC. The ruins of Nevalı Çori near Göbekli Tepe on the Middle Euphrates have been carbon-dated to between 8400 and 8100 BC. The ruins of Tell Hassuna on the Tigris river in Northern Iraq have been carbon-dated to between 7750 and

6780 BC. This naturally leads to the question of why people were building cities in the Levant and Northern Mesopotamia, but nothing in Southern Mesopotamia, even though the region was more climatically stable then, than during the apparently later Sumerian civilization.

If the history of the Egyptian civilization is returned to the longer timeline used by historians and Egyptologists for thousands of years, then the early dynastic period of Sumer would date to circa 7500 BC. This allows both the Sumerian dynastic records to correlate with the Ubaid era ruins and both to co-exist with the later periods of neighboring civilizations to the north and west.

Sumero-Akkadian Timeline

	SUMERO-AKKADIAN TIMELINE	
DYNASTY	**CMT**	**ULT**
1st Kish	2900 to 2800 BC (?)	25,179 to 7698 BC
1st Uruk	2800 to 2700 BC (?)	9868 to 7558 BC
1st Ur	2700 to 2600 BC (?)	7558 to 7381 BC
Awan	2700 to 2600 BC (?)	7381 to 7025 BC
2nd Kish	2700 to 2600 BC (?)	7025 to 4998 BC
Hamazi	2600 to 2500 BC (?)	4998 to 4638 BC
2nd Uruk	2500 to 2400 BC (?)	4638 to 4451 BC
2nd Ur	2500 to 2400 BC (?)	4451 to 4283 BC
Adab	2500 to 2400 BC (?)	4283 to 4193 BC
Mari	2500 to 2400 BC (?)	4193 to 4057 BC
3rd Kish	2500 to 2400 BC (?)	4057 to 3957 BC
Akshak	2500 to 2300 BC (?)	3957 to 3864 BC
4th Kish	2500 (?) to 2359 BC	3864 to 3765 BC
3rd Uruk	2359 to 2334 BC	3910 to 3885 BC
Akkad	2334 to 2154 BC	3885 to 3700 BC

SUMERO-AKKADIAN TIMELINE		
DYNASTY	CMT	ULT
4th Uruk	2244 to 2195 BC	3700 to 3651 BC
Gutian	2195 to 2119 BC	3651 to 3575 BC
5th Uruk	2119 to 2112 BC	3575 to 3568 BC
3rd Ur	2112 to 2004 BC	3568 to 3462 BC
Isin	2017 to 1788 BC	3462 to 3227 BC

The fundamental problem with changing the timeline of Egypt is that Egypt is the only ancient civilization that has a long history that is generally understood, in many cases down to the decade. Therefore, Egypt is used as the metric against which other ancient civilizations are dated. If we didn't have Egypt, other ancient civilizations would exist at unclear points in time, at least in theory. With carbon dating, dendrochronology, and paleoclimatology, we could establish a timeline without Egypt, unfortunately, we have Egypt. Unfortunate, because the existence of the Egyptian timeline forces every other civilization into specific points in time, that generally do not fit the scientific evidence.

While there are many possible mentions of Egypt in Sumerian and Akkadian literature in the earliest periods, none mention anyone specific until the 13th Dynasty of Egypt. During the 13th Dynasty, a stela of Governor Yantinu of Byblos indicates that King Neferhotep I was contemporary with kings Zimri-Lim of the city-state of Mari, and Hammurabi of the Old Babylonian Empire. As the CET places the 13th Dynasty's existence between approximately 1803 to

1649 BC, with Neferhotep I reigning sometime around 1747 to 1736 BC,[1] then both Zimri-Lim and Hammurabi must have reigned around that time.

There is significant physical evidence for the conventional dates being very wrong, and it isn't new. In 1980 Henry Wright published a paper called *Problems of absolute timeline in protohistoric Mesopotamia* that dealt with this issue. The paper's introduction began with the eloquent statement:

> *"Though scholars are seeking to answer increasingly precise questions, about ancient Mesopotamian economic and political developments, the chronological frame of reference which they must use, is not significantly more precise than it was forty years ago.*
>
> *This dilemma has been recently emphasized by James Mellaart. He begins his argument, with reconsiderations of the evidence and reasoning, supporting both the Egyptian and Mesopotamian earlier dynastic timelines, proposing that for both sequences, much earlier datings are defensible.*
>
> *He then considers the carbon 14 age determinations, corrected to approximate actual calendrical dates from Mesopotamia, Anatolia, Egypt, and the Levant. These datings, he argues, also support much older absolute timeline for protohistoric south west Asia proposal, will be criticized by many specialists.*
>
> *It is my purpose here, to look critically at the archaeological use of carbon 14 age*

---

[1] Donald B. Redford, editor (2001) "Egyptian King List," *The Oxford Encyclopedia of Ancient Egypt*, Volume 2. Pages 626-628

> *determinations, from greater Mesopotamian sites of the early fourth to early third millennia BC, in an effort to suggest ways of improving our absolute timeline from this limited region."*

Wright ultimately concluded that there were not enough carbon-dated artifacts from Egypt and Mesopotamia to reconstruct a timeline independent from the historic method used by Egyptologists and Assyriologists in his time. Unfortunately, the situation has not changed much since 1980. There have been multiple attempts to create an Egyptian timeline based on carbon-dating, however, any attempts by non-Egyptologists to alter the conventional timeline by more than a century or two have been completely ignored. Nevertheless, Wright did point out that there were many inconsistencies known even back in 1980. The paper by James Mallaart that Wright referenced was published a year earlier: Egyptian and Near Eastern timeline: A dilemma?[2] It began with the following introduction:

> *"There exists a widespread belief among historians that radiocarbon dating is incompatible with the historical timelines of Egypt and Mesopotamia. In this article the author, lecturer in Anatolian archaeology at the Institute of Archaeology, University of London, attempts to show that a high historical timeline is required by re-interpretation of the Uruk and Jemdet Nasr sequences and their links with Egypt. A comparison with dendrochronology-corrected radiocarbon dating suggests that it is compatible with a high historical timeline. By*

---

[2] James Mellaart (1979) "Egyptian and Near Eastern timeline: A dilemma?" *Antiquity*, 53(207), Pages 6-18

combining these two independent forms of dating it becomes possible to reconstruct a uniform time scale."

In the 1980s and 1990s, there were many attempts to correct the dating of the earlier dynastic periods of Egypt to a long-timeline, however, Egyptologists provided a large number of reasons to dismiss the scientist's findings. One of the best arguments against accepting the older dates that carbon-14 was indicating was that the Egyptians reused materials when they built newer buildings. Therefore, just because a piece of wood used to build a temple might be centuries older than when the temple is believed to have been built by Egyptologists using the CET, these Egyptologists can dismiss the data, as the Egyptians probably built all their temples with wood that had been lying around for centuries. It is a claim that cannot be disproved scientifically.

The problem with changing the Egyptian timeline to ULT is that all other cultures that traded with Egypt need to fit into the ULT. If the Old Kingdom was circa 4945 to 4003 BC, then the Sumerian Civilization would have to date to around the same time, as we know they traded with each other. The city of Uruk should specifically show the earlier dating, as it is generally regarded as being the first major city in Sumer. Until the time of Saddam Hussein, the southern region of Iraq was a marshland, where ancient cities rose above the surrounding waters on what appear to be either terraced hills or artificial mounds. This meant that land was always scarce in the ancient Sumerian cities, and as result buildings were routinely rebuilt.

On the next page is a photograph of an Iraqi marshland town taken in the 1970s. The mound that Uruk was built on, has 13 known distinct periods of construction, each one earlier than the previous as we dig deeper into the mound. Assyriologists date the buildings from Uruk 13 period to circa 5000 BC CMT. Clearly, the earliest Urukians could not have been trading with the Egyptians if the 1st Dynasty of Egypt wasn't founded until 3100 BC CET, yet the earliest Urukians were building flat-topped ziggurats, virtually identical to the mastabas of the 1st and 2nd Dynasties in Egypt. On the next page is a photograph of a mastaba from Saqqara, Egypt, dating from circa 2686 to 2613 BC CET (5247 to 4945 ULT).

One of the main reasons that Assyriologists and Egyptologists believe that Sumer and Egypt were in contact from the earliest periods of their respective histories, is due to the similarity of their scripts. Both the Egyptian hieroglyphs and Sumerian cuneiform combine logographic, syllabic, and alphabetic elements in the same way that few other systems have.

Sumerian cuneiform emerged in Sumer during the Late Uruk period between 3400 and 3100 BC CMT (5231 to 4931 BC ULT). An earlier phase of proto-writing has been discovered dating from at least the Late Ubaid period circa 4500 to 4000 BC CMT (6331 to 5831 BC ULT), which appears to have evolved into cuneiform. This earlier proto-writing period used the same pictographic symbols as early Sumerian, vaguely similar to hieroglyphics. Unfortunately, few examples have been found, and it has not been translated.

Ubaid	Sumerian	Akkadian	Old Babylonian	Neo-Babylonian	
					god, heaven, star, An (Anu)
					Earth, earth, land
					man
					woman
					mountain
					female slave
					head
					mouth
					bread

Meanwhile, hieroglyphics had been under development in Egypt beginning as a pictographic script starting in the pre-dynastic era, in a time period called Naqada III circa 3200 to 3100 BC CET (5610 to 5510 BC ULT), which directly preceded the 1st Dynasty. The earliest hieroglyphics sentence to have been deciphered dates to the 2nd Dynasty, from between 2890 and 2686 BC CET, (5149 to 4945 BC ULT). In the 1900s when the original Egyptian long-timeline was in use, the fact that the earliest Sumerian script looked like the primitive Egyptian hieroglyphs wasn't a problem, the Egyptians had influenced the development of Sumerian cuneiform.

Once the CET became dominant the situation becomes confusing, as now Sumerian Cuneiform influenced the formation of Egyptian Hieroglyphs, yet the Egyptians decided to copy the older no-longer-used pictographic script instead of Cuneiform as the basis of their Hieroglyphs. Below are a series of pre-Dynastic tokens from the tomb of U-j at Abydos, Egypt, dated to the Amratian period between 4000 and 3500 BC CET (6410 to 5910 BC ULT).

Another reason that the earliest phases of both Sumerian and Egyptian history are believed to have influenced each other is that both cultures built large stone platforms, called mastabas in Egypt, and flat-topped ziggurats in Sumer. In both cultures, the stone platforms evolved into pyramid-like structures, pyramids in Egypt, and ziggurats in Sumer. The oldest known mastabas in Egypt date to the pre-historic era, however, they were far simpler than those of the dynastic period. During the 1st Dynasty, the construction of mastabas copied the basic house plan and consisted of several rooms. During the 2nd and 3rd Dynasties, the stairway mastaba became common. These mastabas had a sunken burial chamber and a stairway that allowed access to the top of the mastaba.

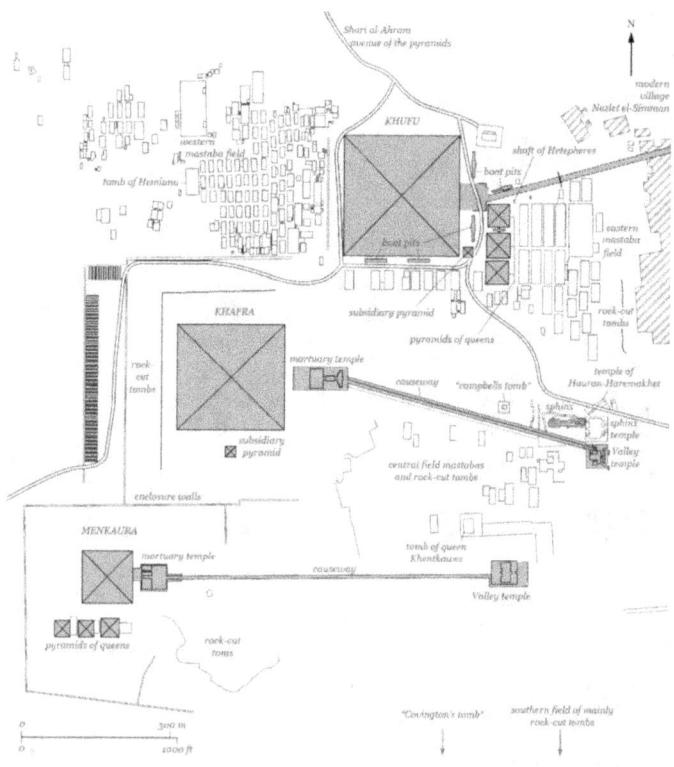

By the 3rd Dynasty, the kings of Egypt had transitioned from building mastabas to pyramids, however, mastabas continued to be used by commoners until the end of the 3rd Dynasty. Hundreds of mastabas were built on the Giza Plateau for nobility and commoners during the 3rd Dynasty, surrounding where the Pyramid of Khufu would later be built. The fact the Western Mastaba Field and Eastern Mastaba Field are built in alignment with the Pyramid of Khufu, which would not be built until the next dynasty has been used by some to suggest that the Pyramid of Khufu was already built by the 3rd Dynasty, and Khufu was at best repairing or rebuilding an older pyramid or mastaba.

On the previous page is a map of the Giza Plateau in Egypt, which shows the Mastaba fields of the 3rd Dynasty build around the 4th Dynasty Pyramid of Khufu. By the 4th Dynasty, the kings were building larger pyramids, reaching a zenith with the Pyramids of Khufu and Khafra on the Giza Plateau, while the nobles and commoners were either building small pyramids or tombs cut into rock cliffs. This means that the mastabas were built from the late pre-dynastic period to the end of the 3rd Dynasty, circa 3200 to 2613 BC CET (or 5610 to 4731 BC ULT).

In Mesopotamia, the oldest known flat-topped ziggurats date back to the Ubaid period between 6500 and 4000 BC CMT (8331 to 5831 BC ULT). By 3000 BC, the Mesopotamian and Iranian Plateau ziggurats were being built in a pyramidal shape, as evidenced by the ziggurat of Tepe Sialk, in the modern city of Kashan, Iran. On the next page is a photo of the ruins of Tepe Sialk in Iran, the oldest known surviving pyramidal ziggurat. It's unclear when the Sumerians transitioned to building pyramidal ziggurats from flat-topped ziggurats, as the humid conditions of southern Iraq and the fact that the Sumerians had limited land, caused the Sumerian ziggurats to be repeatedly rebuilt.

Therefore, the time period when Mesopotamians were building flat-topped pyramids ranged sometime between 6500 and 3000 BC CMT or 9510 to 3000 BC ULT, while the Egyptians were building mastabas between either 3200 and 2613 BC CET or 5610 and 4731 BC ULT. This means that the Mesopotamians were either shifting from flat-topped to pyramidal ziggurats around the time that the Egyptians started to build mastabas according to the conventional timelines, or the two civilizations were building raised platforms and then pyramidal structures around the same time using the ULT.

The Egyptians and Sumerians also began building with the same niched facades during the pre-Dynastic era. In Egypt, niched facade construction began during the Amratian Culture circa 4000 to 3500 BC

CET (6410 to 5910 BC ULT), and was discontinued by the end of the Third Dynasty, circa 2686 to 2613 BC CET (4945 to 4731 BC ULT). In Mesopotamia, niched facade construction began during the Late Uruk period circa 3400 to 3100 BC CMT, and was discontinued during the Jamdet Nasr period circa 3100 to 2900 BC CMT.

Above is a photograph of the ruins of Shunet El-Zebib, in Abydos, Egypt, dated to the 2nd Dynasty, dated to between 2890 and 2686 BC CET (5247 to 4945 BC ULT), which shows the surviving lowest level's niched facade. Fortunately, the lowest level was buried in sand for thousands of years, allowing the original facade to survive the passage of time. The upper levels have been heavily damaged by sandstorms since the original construction. The next image is a photo of the surviving niched facade on the lower level of the Uruk Ziggurat.

As there are no clear parallels between the archaeological and dynastic periods, or delineation between the dynastic and pre-dynastic period in Sumer like there are in Egypt, correlating the two timelines using the prevalence of niched facade construction seems valid. If both cultures were building with niched facades at the same time and stopped around the same time, then the end of the 3rd Dynasty circa 4731 BC ULT would date the end of the Jemdet Nasr period to circa 4731 BC ULT. Using the conventional timelines, the niched facade construction design was used in Egypt between 4000 and 2613 BC, and in Sumer between 3400 to 2900 BC. While in ULT, the niched facade construction design was used in Egypt between 6410 and 4731 BC, and in Sumer between 5231 to 4731 BC.

Generally, the ULT does correlate well with the

Ubaid and Sumerian periods of Mesopotamian history. However, there is the question of the correlation of Egypt's King Neferhotep I and King Zimri-Lm of Mari, and King Hammurabi of Babylon. The CET places the reign of Neferhotep I sometime between 1747 to 1736 BC and 1705 to 1694 BC[3] depending on the version of the CET used. King Zimri-Lim of Mari's reign is dated to circa 1775 to 1761 BC, as this correlates with the life of King Neferhotep I. King Hammurabi's reign is dated to somewhere between 1933 and 1890 BC to 1696 and 1654 BC depending on the version of the CMT used. In both timelines, there are various different versions compiled by different historians. The five dominant chronologies of the CMT are known as the Ultra-Long, Long, Medium, Short, and Ultra-Short timelines. These timelines allow for up to a 250-year fluctuation of the dating of Mesopotamian history. The Middle Chronology is used for the CMT dates here.

Dating the life of King Neferhotep I using the ULT means placing the life of Neferhotep I significantly earlier, between 3246 and 3092 BC. This means that the lives of King Zimri-Lim of Mari and King Hammurabi of Babylon also needs to be moved back to an earlier period. This also means that Mari and Babylon need to have existed at the time. The dating of the Mesopotamian civilization, like the Egyptian Civilization, is subject to gaps where dark ages interrupted civilization. As the Egyptian history was compiled before the Sumerian civilization was even discovered, Assyriologists have traditionally used the Egyptian timeline as a baseline to set the

---

[3] Thomas Schneider (2002) *Lexikon der Pharaonen*

dating for the Sumerian and Akkadian dynasties.

The Mesopotamian timeline is divided into four distinct time periods: the Sumerian, Akkadian, Babylonian, and Late eras. The oldest era is the Sumerian era, which Assyriologists date to between approximately 2900 to 2334 BC CET. These dates were invented to correlate the Sumerian civilization with the Egyptian Early and Old Kingdom eras, as the two cultures were clearly trading extensively at the time. In order to fit the over 21,000 years of recorded Sumerian civilization into the less than 600 years allotted by Assyriologists most of it has to be ignored. Like the Egyptians, the Sumerians recorded a series of dynasties that ruled from different cities, with the kingship passing between the cities as the dynasties changed. In order to try to force the Sumerian civilization into a period of less than 600-years, Assyriologists have had to dismiss the Sumerian claims that the dynasties were in sequence, and assume that they were all happening at the same time. While this may work for most of the dynasties, three of them are more than 600 years long: the 1st Kish Dynasty, the 1st Uruk Dynasty, and the 2nd Kish Dynasty. Therefore these dynasties are simply assumed to be exaggerated by Assyriologists.

The idea that we should dismiss the recorded histories of the Sumerians, Assyrians, Armenians, and other Mesopotamian peoples came from the same source as the idea that we should ignore thousands of years of Egyptian history: James Henry Breasted. On the previous page is a photograph from 1920 of Breasted at the ruins of the Ziggurat of Ur, built by the Neo-Sumerian King Ur-Namma, whose live is dated to circa 2112 to 2092 BC CMT (3568 to 3550 BC ULT). While Breasted is considered an Egyptologist, and not an Assyriologist, he is the source of the CET, and used his position as the founder and first head of the Oriental Institute to push the CET chronology into Assyriology and Indology through the 1920s.

The Oriental Institute was established by Breasted in 1919 with funding from John D. Rockefeller Jr. and the University of Chicago. In the early 1920s, the Oriental Institute funded expeditions to Egypt, Iraq, Syria, Palestine (Israel), and India. In 1923, Breasted became the first archaeologist to be elected to membership in the National Academy of Sciences, and as of 1926, he served as the president of the History of Science Society. That he was influential in the development of Archaeology as an academic field in America cannot be doubted, however, he was also a Christian fundamentalist that insisted on dating civilizations according to the Biblical timeline. He was the source of the currently ubiquitous conventional Egyptian timeline, which he resurrected after it had previously been proposed and disproved in Europe during the 1800s. Unfortunately, the records of the Egyptians and Sumerians do not fit into the Biblical timeline in which the world was created circa 4000 BC, and therefore those ancient human historical records have been both dismissed and even discredited by so-called Egyptologists and Assyriologists.

As the Sumerians rebuilt their cities repeatedly, and the Akkadians and Babylonians that later lived in them rebuilt them as well, very little remains from the Sumerian era, making dismissing the *Sumerian King List* fairly easy. The situation is further complicated by the fact that most of the work done into Mesopotamian history took place during the Ottoman, British, and Ba'athist rules' of Iraq, which were punctuated by World War 1, World War 2, the Republican Revolution, the Iran-Iraq War, the Desert Storm Wars, the US-led Sanctions, the 2003 Invasion of Iraq, and subsequent occupation of Iraq.

Regardless of when the Sumerian civilization existed, the ruins in Iraq are far older than 2900 BC. Assyriologists classify the earlier eras as the Ubaid, Uruk, and Jamdet Nasr eras, and date them to between 6500 BC CMT and the beginning of the dynastic era. If the Egyptian Old Kingdom wasn't dated to circa 2686 to 2181 BC CET, these earlier periods of Iraqi ruins would be considered Sumerian. These ruins are in the same cities that the Sumerians later lived in, including Uruk, Ur, and Eridu, yet these ruins cannot be dated to the Sumerian civilization, as the Sumerians were trading with the Egyptians early in their civilization.

If the ULT is used for the Egyptian civilization, and the end of the Jemdet Nasr era is synchronized with the end of the Egyptian 3rd Dynasty, then the Ubaid, Uruk, and Jemdet Nasr eras would span the period of circa 8331 to 4731 BC, permitting almost all of the dynasties after the first dynasty to exist within known ruins. The second dynasty on the Sumerian King Lists was the 1st Uruk Dynasty which would span the time period of 9868 to 7558 BC ULT. The first dynasty was the 1st Kish Dynasty, which spanned the time period of 25,179 to 7698 BC ULT. Nothing survives from the 1st Kish Dynasty, even the location of Kish is unknown, however, it is believed to be somewhere in the region of Babylon. As the 1st Kish Dynasty cannot be proven to have existed by any currently known archaeological evidence, it is best to deal with it as a pre-Dynastic period, along with the Antediluvian period on the Sumerian King Lists.

Before 7000 BC, most of southern Iraq would have been dry land, however by 6000 BC the region was beginning to flood as the water level in the region rose after the Persian Gulf flooded. Throughout most of the Last Glacial Period, the Persian Gulf was exposed land, as the region only averages around 35 meters below modern sea level, and the oceans fell to as low as 135 meters below modern sea level. The Persian Gulf flooded between 10,000 and 7000 BC, following which the southern region of Iraq began flooding, creating the wetland that Sumer was built in.

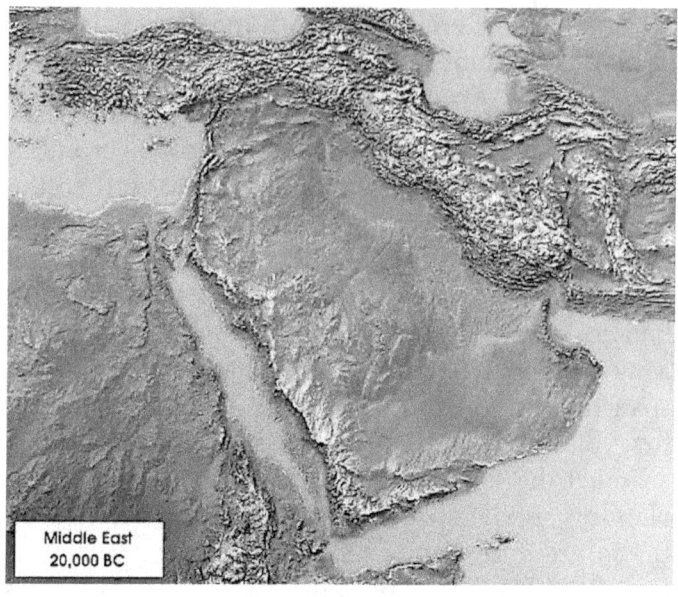

Middle East
20,000 BC

The fact that Sumer was built in a wetland should itself point to the civilization being older than the wetland, as civilizations aren't generally built in swamps. The oldest phases of construction in Uruk, from before the Uruk 5 period, includes the use of large amounts of limestone and bitumen, while after Uruk 5 the Sumerians switched to building with abode bricks. Building with adobe in a wetland makes some sense, as they would have had access to mud, however, the limestone is a mystery, as the Sumerians did not have a local source of stone, which was one of their major imported commodities. Importing enough stone to build the base of a ziggurat is a hopelessly illogical concept, yet it is a requisite of the CMT. Clearly, the earliest Urukians had access to locally sourced limestone, which would mean they were quarrying in the region prior to the water level rising after 7000 BC.

Using this longer timeline for the Sumerian civilization also allows the Sumerian King Lists to make sense, as they claimed that King Gilgamesh reigned around 3900 years before King Sargon, who is traditionally dated to around 2300 BC CET, however, would date to approximately 3850 BC ULT. One problem with allowing the Sumerian civilization to span the length of the Ubaid period is that we have no clay tablets from the Ubaid period that show signs of writing, however, that does not mean that they were not writing.

The invention of the clay tablet as a form of record may have been a late invention and would have naturally led to the use of a standardized impression tool, and ultimately a new writing system, which we call cuneiform. For the Sumerians, the invention of the clay tablet would have been as revolutionary as the invention of movable type was to the Europeans in the 1400s. Movable type standardized calligraphy and enforced the use of the Latin alphabet across western Europe. Over the following centuries, cultures that did not use the Latin alphabet slowly fell behind technologically and socially, as ideas could not move as freely in those cultures.

The pictographs on the Ubaid era imprint indicates that the seal dates to at least the Late Ubaid era, circa 4500 to 4000 BC CMT (6331 to 5831 BC ULT). Below is a similar imprint from the Akkadian era showing Ea, the Akkadian Enki (center), and Usumu, the Akkadian Isinu, (right). The Akkadian era seal dates to after 2334 BC CMT (3885 BC ULT), indicating that while Assyriologists may not want to accept the fact that the Ubaid ruins are Sumerian, the Ubaidians did worship the same gods as the Sumerians and Akkadians.

Above is a Ubaid era seal imprint depicting the water-god Enki (center) and the two-faced messenger-god Isinu (right). On the next page is a Babylonian seal impression of the same gods. The Egyptians were using papyrus from at least the 1st Dynasty, and as the two cultures were trading ideas about how to build massive stone platforms and then pyramids, it seems likely someone would have introduced papyrus to Sumer. The fact that we don't find papyrus in the ruins of Ubaid is not proof that they didn't use papyrus as Ubaid was built in marshland, while Egypt was built along a river, surrounded by what became desert after 6000 years ago.

Even in Egypt, we find virtually no surviving papyrus until the Middle Kingdom. We do find some, so we know they were using it, but we find very little. In Ubaid, the climate would have caused the papyrus to rot within centuries, and would naturally explain why they ultimately invented the clay tablet. In Egypt, when they wanted to create a document that would last a long time, they carved it into stone, however, the Sumerians had very little stone, and in fact, it was one of their main imports. Carving records into stone would have been far too expensive when they were surrounded by the exact same reeds the Egyptians used to make papyrus.

The development of Sumerian clay tablets has been traced back directly to Ubaid era clay tokens called bullae, which began to be used between 8,000 and 7,500 BC. These bullae represented grain and livestock which were often stored in communal facilities due to the limited amount of land available in the Ubaid cities. They also appear to have been used in trade, as a type of proto-money. The bullae remained virtually unchanged for over 4000 years, until approximately 4000 to 3500 BC, when they began to become more elaborate.

Ubaid Bulla	Sumerian Pictograph	Akkadian Cuneiform	Neo-Assyrian Cuneiform	Neo-Babylonian Cuneiform	Meaning
					Sheep
					Cattle
					Dog
					Metal
					Oil
					Garment
					Braclet
					Perfume

Above is a diagram showing the evolution of bullae into cuneiform. During the Sumerian dynastic and later periods in Mesopotamia, bullae were accompanied by papyrus that explained their value, for example: 'this bulla is worth two cows at the livestock holding pen.' This made them more like a bankers' check than true money in the modern concept, however very much like early paper money that was once backed by gold. It is difficult to comprehend how the bullae could have ever been used without papyrus explaining what they were valued at, and is, therefore, a strong indicator that papyrus, and writing, were used in Mesopotamia since the introduction of the bulla circa 8000 to 7500 BC.

While Sumerian cuneiform is documented to have evolved out of Ubaid bullae, the two scripts are both used on the Daily Salary tablet AO 20052 at the Louvre, pictured below. As there is no reason for the two scripts to have been written at the same time, this indicates that the Sumerians were copying older Ubaid era tablets, much as later Mesopotamian civilizations would copy Sumerian texts.

The third period in the Mesopotamian timeline is the Akkadian era, which is also derived from the Sumerian King Lists and is a direct continuation from the Sumerian era. The Akkadian people are believed to have settled in the Sumerian civilization and eventually become dominant. King Sargon was the first Akkadian King, who overthrew the last Sumerian King and established the Akkadian Empire, eventually gaining control over all of the former Sumerian territories. This civilization generally continued the Sumerian civilization, however, the dominant language shifted to Akkadian, the ancestral language of Babylonian and Assyrian. The Akkadians continued to live in the Sumerian cities, and rebuild them, and therefore there are more Akkadian era relics than Sumerian or Ubaid.

Unlike the earlier Sumerians, the Akkadians were a Semitic people, whose language served as the basis of both the Old Babylonian and Old Assyrian languages.[4] Both Old Babylonian and Old Assyrian are very closely related to Akkadian, sometimes being classified as dialects of Akkadian, however, they are easily distinguishable from both each other and Akkadian. Both the Babylonians and Assyrians adopted Akkadian cuneiform for their written records, which for the Babylonians isn't a problem, as they conquered the Akkadians, however, it is a problem for the Assyrians. The Assyrians had records of their people's history long preceding the foundation of the Old Assyrian Empire, circa 1905 BC CMT (3278 BC ULT). This earlier period is known as the Early Assyrian Period, which either spans

---

[4] Richard Caplice (1980) *Introduction to Akkadian*

2447 to 1906 BC CMT, or 3764 to 3278 BC ULT. As this period must have happened after the Akkadian Empire circa 2334 to 2154 BC CMT (3885 to 3700 BC ULT), it is generally ignored by Assyriologists as it begins over a century before the Akkadian Empire was founded in the CMT. In the ULT, the Early Assyrian Period began late in the Akkadian Empire, with the foundation of the Old Assyrian Empire happening near the end of the Neo-Sumerian Empire. Again this is a strong indicator that the conventional timelines are wrong as we either have to ignore the records of the Assyrians, or accept they were time-travelers to make their history fit into the CMT.

Babylonian Timeline

BABYLONIAN TIMELINES		
PERIOD	CMT	ULT
Old Babylonian Empire	1894 to 1595 BC	3352 to 3038 BC
Kassite Dynasty	1570 to 1155 BC	3013 to 1155 BC
Elamite Empire	1210 to 1100 BC	1210 to 1100 BC
Neo-Assyrian Empire	912 to 612 BC	912 to 612 BC
Neo-Babylonian Empire	612 to 539 BC	612 to 539 BC

The fourth period in the Mesopotamian timeline is the Late Era, which includes the Babylonian, Assyrian, and later civilizations. The Babylonian timeline is derived from the Babylonian King Lists and continues where the Sumerian King Lists end. The Babylonian civilization was largely a continuation of the Akkadian civilization, however, the capital city of Babylon was north of the marshlands. The fact that the Babylonian King Hammurabi was around at the same time as the Egyptian King Neferhotep I requires moving the entire Old Babylonian Empire to circa 3352 to 3038 BC ULT.

This does not affect the dating of the later periods, as there was a dark age after the Fall of Babylon at the end of the Old Babylonian Empire. The Hittite sacking of Babylon is considered one of the most important events in the Babylonian timeline and generally dated to somewhere between 1499 and 1736 BC depending on the version of the CMT used. If the

ULT is used then the Fall of Babylon took place around 3038 BC, around 200 years after the collapse of the Egyptian Middle Kingdom. The ULT also sees the reign of the last Neo-Sumerian King, Damiq-il-ishu, ending in 3227 BC, around the same time the Egyptian Middle Kingdom collapsed, shortly after the Great Shock of 3250 BC. This is the point in time that the world's climate changed significantly into a neo-glacial period that lasted until around 1500 BC.

There are a number of pieces of evidence supporting the existence of this Great Shock of 3250 BC. During this time the world's weather became stormier, and there was far more rain, which would have caused significant flooding along the Tigris and Euphrates, and significant flooding of the Mesopotamian marshlands, as well as along other rivers and in other swamps throughout the world.[5] The GISP2 ice core samples from Greenland show there was a spike in atmospheric sulfate at 3250 BC, believed to have been from an increasing number of polynyas in the Arctic, caused by an expansion of oceanic surface ice.[6] The GRIP ice core sample from Greenland shows the 3250 BC point as being at a low point in atmospheric methane, followed by a rapid increase over the next 200 years, which is attributed to an abrupt increase in global wetlands.[7] Ice core samples from the Huascaran glacier in Peru, show

[5] Lisa L. Ely, et al. (October 15, 1993) "A 5000-Year Record of Extreme Floods and Climate Change in the Southwestern United States," *Science*, New Series, Volume 262, Number 5132, Pages 410-412

[6] G. A. Zielinski, et al. (1994) *Nature*, Volume 264, Page 948

[7] T. Blunier, et al. (1995) *Nature*, Volume 374, Page 47

an abrupt cooling at about 3250 BC.[8]

It is a historical fact that the Hittites sacked Babylon at the end of the reign of the Old Babylonian King Samsu-Ditana. Babylonia was left in a state of anarchy, and around 24 years later a people called the Kassites occupied Babylonia, and rebuilt the city, renaming it Karduniash. The Kassites ruled Babylonia for centuries, however, they left very little in the way of records until the 1300s BC. This time period is called the Babylonian Dark Age, or Mesopotamian Dark Age, as there are very few records of the time from Babylonia, Elam, Assyria, the Hittite Empire, and Canaan. This dark age either took place between 1524 and 1373 BC CMT, or 2965 and 1373 BC ULT. This means it either happened after the Second Egyptian Dark Age (Second Intermediate Period), which was between 1803 and 1549 BC CET, or it happened at the same time as the Second Egyptian Dark Age between 3246 and 1580 BC ULT.

If the Babylonian Dark Age happened after the Second Egyptian Dark Age, then there is no dark age, as the timeline of the Old Kingdom Assyrians can be continued in the New Kingdom Egyptians. Theoretically, there should be no inconsistencies if both conventional timelines are correct, however, there is the massive anachronism of the Hyksos, a Semitic and Hurrian people, that used Indo-Aryan words and technology, who invaded Egypt circa 1674 BC CET. According to the Egyptians the Hyk-

---

[8] L. G. Thompson, et al. (July 7, 1995) "Late Glacial Stage and Holocene Tropical IceCore Records from Huascaran, Peru," *Science*, Volume 269, Pages 46-50

sos invaded Egypt from the Middle East after conquering Canaan, yet according to the CMT, they were not there, or anywhere. Indo-Aryans didn't enter the Middle East until after the Sack of Babylon circa 1595 BC CMT. This is as clear as any evidence could be that the conventional timelines are wrong. In the ULT, Babylon was sacked in 3038 BC and the Hyksos occupied Egypt in 2533 BC, explaining why Indo-Aryan words were being used by a Semitic and Hurrian people.

Placing the Old Babylonian Empire in the ULT does not affect the later periods of the Mesopotamian timeline, however, it does affect the earlier Sumerian and Akkadian Periods. The Sumerian King List provides a continual list of king spanning thousands of years of history. If the Fall of Babylon was circa 3038 BC, then the life of Sargon of Akkad would date to circa 3885 to 3845 BC, and the life of Gilgamesh would date to between 7824 and 7698 BC, assuming all of the dynasties are in sequence other than the known dynastic overlaps. Assyriologists don't generally consider the dynasties to have actually been sequential, as they have been forced to compress all of Dynastic history into a period of only a few hundred years, in order to synchronize it with the CET.

Correlating the life of Hammurabi with the life of Neferhotep I according to the ULT is not problematic, however correlating the life of Zimri-Lim of Mari to circa 3230 BC, is a problem as Mari is generally regarded as being founded in 2900 BC. Unlike many other Sumerian cities, Mari did not start as some little village that grew into a larger city, it was founded as a colonial city during the Mesopotamian Early Dynastic period I. This however also resolves the issue, because if the Old Babylonian Empire was circa 3352 to 3038 BC, then the Mesopotamian Early Dynastic period I would have been thousands of years earlier, and according to the ULT interpretation of the Sumerian King List, existed by 4200 BC.

Assyrian Timeline

ASSYRIAN TIMELINES		
PERIOD	**CMT**	**ULT**
Early Assyrian Period	2447 to 1906 BC	3764 to 3278 BC
Old Assyrian Empire	1905 to 1517 BC	3278 to 2965 BC
Mitanni Empire	1590 to 1460 BC	2967 to 1460 BC
Middle Assyrian Kingdom	1460 to 912 BC	
Neo-Assyrian Empire	912 to 612 BC	

Synchronizing the timelines of the Middle East with the ULT also means synchronizing the timeline of the Assyrians. Like the Babylonian civilization in central Mesopotamia, the Assyrian civilization in northern Mesopotamia developed out of the Akkadian culture. The historic periods of the Assyrian civilization are divided into five eras, the Early Assyrian Period, the Old Kingdom, the Mitanni rule, the Middle Kingdom, and the Neo-Assyrian Empire. Linguistically the Assyrian language developed from the Akkadian language, meaning the Akkadian civilization should precede the Assyrian civilization, however in the CMT, the Early Assyrian Period actually preceded the Akkadian Empire. How the Assyrians adopted Akkadian cuneiform, instead of Sumerian cuneiform is not explained by Assyriologists. In the ULT the Assyrian Early Period starts near the end of the Akkadian Empire, which explains why the Assyrians adopted Akkadian cuneiform.

In the CMT, the founder of the Assyrian dynasty, Tudiya, existed roughly a century before Sargon, the founder of the Akkadian Empire, while in the ULT, Tudiya lived around a century after Sargon. As Tudiya could not have lived before Sargon, when the CMT was compressed to synchronize it with the CET, Tudiya and the entire Early Assyrian Period was discredited and demoted from history to mythology. The ancient Assyrians recorded the Early Assyrian Period as a record of the history of the 'kings who lived in tents,' meaning the Assyrians were still nomadic at the time and hadn't yet settled in the land later known as Assyria.

The Old Assyrian Kingdom timeline ran parallel to the Old Babylonian Empire and was for a while under the dominion of the Old Babylonian Empire after Hammurabi ousted the Assyrian King Ishme-Dagan I, and forced his son King Mut-Ashkur to pay tribute. Assyria continued as an independent kingdom for some time after the destruction of Babylon, slowly or quickly losing territory to the rising Mitanni Empire, and then fell under the dominion of the Mitanni Empire entirely, which they didn't break lose of until the beginning of the Middle Kingdom era, sometime before the Egyptian New Kingdom destroyed the Mitanni army in the Battle of Megiddo. The Mitanni Empire rose during the Babylonian dark age, which in the ULT, corresponds with the Second Egyptian Dark Age in Egypt. The people of the Mitanni Empire were mostly Hurrian, with an Indo-Aryan nobility, and appear to be the source of the Hyksos that occupied Egypt during the Second

Egyptian Dark Age, who were mostly Semitic, but with a Hurrian nobility, and who used Indo-Aryan words.

The Mitanni occupied the region that corresponds to modern Syria, creating the Mitanni Empire within a century of the Sack of Babylon, seizing territory from the Hittites to the north, and Assyrians to the east. In the CMT the empire was established by 1560 BC when they sacked the Assyrian capital of Ashur, while in the ULT the empire was established by 2967 BC when they occupied Yamhad. This was during the Babylonian dark age, so few records survive. It is known that the Mitanni Empire either very quickly or gradually conquered the Assyrian Empire, however, it had lost control of Assyria sometime before the Battle of Megiddo circa 1457 BC. While the surviving records seem to indicate that the wars between the Mitanni and Assyrians lasted for centuries before the fall of Ashur, the fact that the Assyrian timeline needs to synchronize with the CET forces Assyriologists to accept the premise that the Mitanni conquered, ruled and then lost Assyria between circa 1560 and 1457 BC CMT. In the ULT this is a long sequence of events that took place between 2967 and 1457 BC ULT, in fact, it is unclear when Assyria regained its independence from the Mitanni, and they could have been independent for centuries by the time of the Battle of Meggido. All that is known is that the Assyrians were independent at the time of the Battle of Megiddo, as they, along with the Babylonians and Hittites, sent tribute to King Thutmose III after he defeated the Mitanni army.

Synchronizing the Assyrian timeline with the

ULT doesn't create any issues, as the Assyrian time-line has a dark age after the collapse of the Old King-dom. The Assyrian Dark Age correlates with the Babylonian Dark Age, and the Second Egyptian Dark Age in the ULT. This dark age saw the rise of the Mi-tanni in Syria and the Hyksos in Egypt, two cultures that left very little in terms of written records. After the Egyptians had driven the Egyptianized-Hyksos 16th Dynasty out of Egypt, around 1731 BC ULT, they launched a series of invasions into Canaan, oc-cupying most of the Mediterranean coast of modern Israel/Palestine, Lebanon, and Syria, culminating in the Battle of Megiddo in 1457 BC. The Battle of Megiddo was an insurrection against Egyptian rule led by the Kings of Kadesh and Megiddo, and backed by the Mitanni Empire. It ended with the Egyptian army destroying the Canaanite armies and the 330 princes and tribal leaders of the Mitanni. A few years later the Egyptians launched an invasion of the Mitanni Empire, and were able to enter the capital of Washukanni and capture King Barattarna without encountering a Mitanni Army. While they did not gain any territory from the Mitanni, they did show the weakness of the Mitanni, and by 1228 BC the Mi-tanni Empire effectively ceased to exist, becoming a vassal of the Assyrian Middle Kingdom.

Hittite Timeline

HITTITE TIMELINES		
PERIOD	**CMT**	**ULT**
Old Hittite Empire	1664 to 1524 BC	3103 to 2965 BC
Middle Hittite Kingdom	1524 to 1400 BC	2965 to 1450 BC
New Hittite Empire	1400 to 1178 BC	1450 to 1178 BC

Adjusting the dating of the Egyptian civilization and Old Babylonian Empire to correspond with the ULT, also means adjusting the Hittite Empire's dating. The Hittites sacked Babylon circa 3038 BC ULT and therefore the Hittite civilization needs to have existed by 3038 BC. Like the Egyptian civilization the Hittite civilization is divided into three kingdoms, the Old, Middle, and New Kingdoms. However, these kingdoms are not as ancient as the Egyptian kingdoms. The Hittite Old Kingdom is the Empire that destroyed the Old Babylonian Empire, which means that it had to be around circa 3038 BC.

There is only one known synchronism between the Hittite Old Kingdom and the Old Babylonian Empire, the sacking of Babylon. If this is set to circa 3038 BC, then the era of the Old Kingdom spans approximately 3103 to 2967 BC. The Hittites are believed to have begun migrating into Anatolia from the Balkans sometime between 100 and 200 years before the foundation of the Old Kingdom, placing the migration roughly around the time of the Great Shock of 3250 BC. The Hittite destruction of Babylon under King Mursili I was the Old Kingdom's furthest military reach, and after the lengthy campaign against Babylonia, the Hittite resources were strained, and the capital was left in a state of near-anarchy. King Mursili I was assassinated shortly after returning home, and the Hittite Kingdom fell into a state of chaos. The neighboring Hurrian culture emerged during the chaos to occupy the southern half of the Hittite Kingdom, from the Tigris River to the Mediterranean coast, forming the Mitanni Empire.

The Hittite Old Kingdom fought a series of wars against the Mitanni, however, the Old Kingdom was not able to regain its lost territory, and slowly withered. By the end of the Old Kingdom, circa 2967 BC ULT, the Hittite civilization had been reduced to its core territory in central Anatolia, and virtually no records remain from the time. The Hittite Dark Age that followed is referred to as the Middle Kingdom era. Few records remain from the period, and although the names of some kings are known, it is unclear how long the Middle Kingdom era lasted. There are no synchronisms with either the Egyptian or Mesopotamian civilizations known from the Middle Kingdom. What is known is that there is a list of six kings believed to have ruled sometime during this era, however, even the capital of the kingdom during their rule is unclear, as the besieged Hittites repeatedly moved their capital.

The Hittite New Kingdom emerged by 1457 BC, as they paid tribute to the Egyptians after the Battle of Megiddo. The Hittite New Kingdom also called the New Hittite Empire, is well known from the Egyptian New Kingdom and Assyrian Middle Kingdom records. There is no conflict when the dating of the Hittite New Kingdom on the ULT, as both the Hittite and Egyptian New Kingdoms existed around the same time. This Hittite Empire became a dominant power in Anatolia and Syria during the era of the Egyptian New Kingdom and the Assyrian Middle Kingdom.

Kassite-Mitanni-Hyksos Timeline

KASSITE-MITANNI-HYKSOS TIMELINE			
CIVILIZATION	PERIOD	CMT	ULT
Babylonia	Kassite Dynasty	1570 to 1155 BC	3013 to 1155 BC
Mitanni	Mitanni Empire	1500 to 1300 BC	2967 to 1300 BC
Egypt	Canaanite 14th Dynasty	1674 to 1535 BC	2793 to 2533 BC
Egypt	Hyksos 15th Dynasty	1674 to 1535 BC	2533 to 2249 BC
Egypt	Egyptianized-Hyksos 16th Dynasty	1660 to 1600 BC	2249 to 1731 BC

Synchronizing the Hurrian civilization with the ULT is also required if the ULT is correct. The Hurrians were a people that lived in northern Syria and northern Mesopotamia, first attested during the Akkadian Empire. Sometime after the Hittite destruction of the Old Babylonian Empire, the Hurrians became united under an Indo-Aryan monarchy and forged the Mitanni Empire. This empire formed in the wake of the power vacuum created by the Hittite's conquest of the Kingdom of Yamhab in northern Syria, and the destruction of the Old Babylonian Empire in central Iraq, followed by the collapse of the power structure within the Hittite Empire. The rise of this empire was also possible as the Old Assyrian Empire was in decline at the time.

Very little is actually known about the Mitanni

Empire, or the Hurrian peoples, as there are very few records from the time. The Hurrian people spoke a language related to the language of the Urartu people of the Old Armenian Highlands of eastern modern Turkey and may have been the indigenous people of northern Mesopotamia. The Hurrians were documented as living in northern Mesopotamia during the Akkadian and Old Babylonian Empires, however, did not constitute a separate civilization until the rise of the Mitanni Empire.

The fact that the civilization fell under the control of an Indo-Aryan nobility is strange regardless of when the civilization existed. The homeland of the Indo-Aryan culture is unknown but generally assumed to have been in Central Asia or the Eurasian Steppes. The Indo-Aryans did have quite a lot in common with the Hittites, who were also an Indo-European people, and shared several deities including Indra, Mitra, Nasatya, and Varuna.

During the declining years of the Hittite Old Kingdom, the Mitanni Empire occupied its southern territories, ranging from the Tigris River to the Mediterranean coast of Cilicia. This empire also occupied the western areas of the Assyrian Empire, which was also in decline at the time. In Canaan, the Mitanni occupied several kingdoms including Aziru and Amurru, and turned Alalakh and Kizzuwatna into vassal states. Eventually, the entire Assyrian Empire fell under the dominion of the Mitanni, although when this took place is unknown as both empires left virtually no records during this period. Like the other older civilizations, the Assyrian civilization had gone into rapid decline around the same time as the Hittites and Egyptians, however, had started recovering sometime before the Battle of Megiddo circa 1457 BC.

The Mitanni Empire left very little in terms of written records, however, it was around for either a very short time between 1590 and 1300 BC CMT, or a long time between sometime before 2967 and 1300 BC ULT. The Mitanni left no king lists, and their kings are only known from their interactions with neighboring civilizations. Several synchronizations can be made between the Mitanni kings and the kings of the Egyptian New Kingdom, Assyrian Middle Kingdom, and the Kassite Dynasty of Babylonia. Regardless of the timeline used the Mitanni Empire existed during a dark age.

The Babylonian Dark Age took place at approximately the same time as the Second Egyptian Dark Age, which was either between approximately 1524 and 1460 BC CMT, or 2965 and 1460 BC ULT in Mesopotamia, and between approximately 1803 and 1549 BC CET, or 3246 and 1580 BC ULT in Egypt. Using the ULT these dark ages overlapped, however, using the conventional timelines they don't overlap, which means there should not be a dark age.

The appearance of the Indo-Aryans in the Middle East at the time was not unique to the Mitanni Empire. After the Hittites laid waste to Babylon, Babylonia was occupied by a militant faction of people known as the Kassites, who appear to have had an Indo-Aryan nobility.[9] The Kassites themselves spoke

[9] Robert MacHenry (1992) The new encyclopaedia Britannica: in 32 vol. Macropaedia, India - Ireland, Volume 21. Encyclopedia *Britannica*. Page 36

a language which is only partially understood, as very little appears to have been written in it. The Kassite language has been identified by various linguists as either related to the Hurro-Urartian languages,[10] or the Caucasian languages.[11] These people are believed to have migrated into Babylonia from the Zagros Mountains of northern Iran, sometime after the Hittites destroyed Babylon.

The Kassite Dynasty was one of the longest in Babylonian history, although not popular with the general populace, who saw these Kassites as foreign occupiers. Like the Hyksos in Egypt, the Kassites tried to assimilate into the local culture and used Babylonian as the language of governance and business, however, they were also a brutal military dictatorship. The Kassites occupied Babylon around 1571 BC CMT or 3013 BC ULT, either way around 25 years after the Sack of Babylon.

The appearance of the Indo-Aryan led Kassites, could explain the rise of the Hurrians in northern Mesopotamia around the same time. The Hurrians were in northern Mesopotamia since at least the Akkadian era and could be the aboriginal population of northern Mesopotamia. If the Kassite language was related to the Hurrian and Urartu languages, as the dominant theory currently suggests, then the

---

[10] Thomas Schneider (2003) "Kassitisch und Hurro-Urartäisch. Ein Diskussionsbeitrag zu möglichen lexikalischen Isoglossen," *Altorientalische Forschungen* (30): 372-381

[11] E. D. Phillips (1963) "The Peoples of the Highland: Vanished Cultures of Luristan, Mannai and Urartu," *Vanished Civilizations of the Ancient World.* Page 241

Kassites likely saw the Hurrians, who had been ruled by Akkadians, Babylonians, Assyrians, and Hittites for centuries, as long lost cousins. It is not unreasonable to see the rise of the Mitanni Empire as a Kassite backed plot, if for no other reason than to weaken the other powers in the region. It is well established that the two countries maintained strong relations throughout their existences.

It is unclear when the Hurrians began to rise against the Hittites and Assyrians, as this also happened in the dark age. It is nevertheless depicted in the CMT as happening almost instantaneously, as there isn't much time in the CMT, and the Mitanni had to build an empire that could sack Ashur by 1560 BC, and dominate the Hittites, conquer most of Canaan, then conquer Assyria itself, and then lose it all by 1460 BC. Fortunately, the ULT allows the Hurrians centuries to have built and then lost the Mitanni Empire.

The Hyksos, who invaded Egypt from Syria and Canaan, were a dominantly Semitic people, with a Hurrian nobility, that used Indo-Aryan names and loanwords, as one would expect the Mitanni to have developed into after a few centuries. According to the generally accepted CET, the Hyksos migrated into Egypt starting around 1674 BC, over a century before the Hittite sack of Babylon created the power vacuum that allowed the Kassites to invade Babylonia, and before the Mitanni Empire suddenly materialized from nowhere according to the CMT. In fact, if one accepts the CET, there is no explanation for a Semitic people with a Hurrian nobility using Indo-Aryan words and names originating anywhere in the

Middle East, or anywhere else on Earth. Circa 1674 BC CMT there were the Old Babylonian, Old Hittite, and Old Assyrian Empires dominating the region, with no signs of Indo-Aryans anywhere nearby.

If the ULT is used, then the Egyptian Middle Kingdom collapsed into the Second Egyptian Dark Age starting around 3246 BC. The last of the Neo-Sumerian kings lost power in 3227 BC, likely due to the extensive flooding of the old Iraqi Marshlands caused by the Great Shock of 3250 BC. In the centuries that followed Babylon grew in power as the new focus of trade in Southern and Central Mesopotamia, and new powers rose in the formerly dry northern regions around of Ashur and Hattusa to the north. These northern regions thrived for a couple of centuries before ultimately drying back to their previous conditions as the global climate stabilized. As the crops failed in the north circa 3050 BC, the Hittites began expanding their first Empire, raiding first Yamhad in modern Syria, and then sacking Babylonia circa 3038 BC.

The ULT continues with a group of people known as Kassites migrating down from the Zagros mountains into Babylonia and establishing their rule over the region by 3013 BC. These people were ruled by an Indo-Aryan nobility and used both horses and wagons, a technology believed to have been invented by Indo-Aryans or their predecessors in the Eurasian Steppes or Eastern Europe, sometime before the Bronocice pot was made between 3635 and 3370 BC.[12] The earliest known surviving securely

---

[12] Wozy z Bronocic (2009) *Strona oficjalna Muzeum Archeologicznego z Krakowie*

dated wheel is the Ljubljana Marshes Wheel, from Slovenia, which is carbon-dated to 3150 BC. In the ULT the Kassites introduce the chariot to Mesopotamia circa 3013 BC, and the Hyksos later introduce the chariot to Egypt circa 2533 BC.

In the conventional timelines, the Sumerians were using the horse-drawn chariot since at least 2600 BC, but it was not introduced to Egypt until the Hyksos Dynasty circa 1674 BC. This anachronism is not explained by Egyptologists, who simply accept that the Egyptians lagged almost a thousand years behind the Sumerians technologically by the Egyptian Middle Kingdom, even while they were trading extensively with the Sumerians. The idea that the Egyptians built the Grand Canal and terraced the Fayum depression by hand, instead of using horses and carts to carry away the debris is profoundly illogical, and it seems hopelessly implausible that the ancient Egyptians could have been that stupid.

It is even more absurd that the Sumerians were using horses and wagons during the Egyptian Old Kingdom, and instead of importing the technology, the ancient Egyptians chose to build the great pyramids with brute human strength. Using the conventional timelines the Egyptians and Sumerians exchanged ideas about how to build mastabas and pyramids, and taught each other the art of writing, and even exchanged ideas about mythical animals, but at no point did the Egyptians look at the horse, or even the wheel, and think, 'that might be useful.'

In the ULT the introduction of the wheel into Mesopotamia by the Kassites circa 3013 BC was at the beginning of the Babylonian Dark Age, and only two centuries into the more the 1600 year long Second Egyptian Dark Age. The Indo-Aryan Kassite nobility of Babylon extended their control into Syria, establishing the Mitanni Empire, by seizing control of the native Hurrian population, and using them to subjugate the Amorite population of Canaan. This new Mitanni Empire appears to have been more of a Steppes-style confederation than a Mesopotamian-style kingdom. As demonstrated at the Battle of Megiddo circa 1457 BC, and its aftermath. In the Battle of Megiddo, the Mitanni backed the kings of Kadesh and Megiddo in their attempt to resist Egyptian domination of Canaan. The Mitanni were described as the 330 princes and tribal leaders of the Mitanni, which were destroyed by the Egyptian forces. A few years later when the Egyptians launched an invasion of the Mitanni Empire, they were able to enter the capital of Washukanni and capture King Barattarna without meeting a Mitanni army. This strongly indicates that the Mitanni were not a unified kingdom with a standing army, but rather a confederation of tribes.

By 2793 BC ULT, a group of Canaanites, who had been living in Northern Egypt since the Middle Kingdom, seized power and established the 14th Dynasty. This Dynasty was in turn conquered by the Hyksos around 2533 BC ULT, who formed the 15th Dynasty. The modern name Hyksos is derived from the ancient Egyptian term 'heqa khasut,' which translates as 'rulers of foreign lands.' The term had been used since at least the Middle Kingdom for any foreign government, but this was the first time a foreign government was described as ruling Egypt. Egyptologists do not interpret the Hyksos as being a foreign government, as the Hyksos Dynasty occupied Egypt circa 1674 BC CET, while the Old Babylonian, Old Assyrian, and Old Hittite Empires were still around, and none of them bothered recording that they conquered Egypt, which one of them would have had to have done, as the Egyptians recorded the Hyksos conquering Canaan before entering Egypt.

Instead, Egyptologists cling to the idea proposed by the Jewish Historian Josephus circa 94 AD, that the Hyksos were a group of nomadic 'Shepherd Kings,' even though his etymology of Hyksos as 'Shepherd Kings' has, ironically, been thoroughly discredited by Egyptologists. The fact that the term Hyksos is derived from the ancient Egyptian term for 'foreign ruler' is not disputed by Egyptologists, yet clearly, there were no foreign powers that could have been ruling Egypt circa 1674 BC to 1535 BC CET. Conversely, there was a foreign power circa 2533 BC to 2249 BC ULT that not only could have, by should have conquered the Canaanite Dynasty of Egypt, the Mitanni Empire, who had conquered the Canaanites in Canaan.

The Hyksos formed the 15th Dynasty in Egypt, which in the CET overlaps with the 13th, 16th, Abydos, 17th, and 18th Dynasties in order to compress the timeline. This means that multiple Egyptian dynasties were concurrent in the CET, controlling different regions, and fighting various undocumented wars. In the ULT, these dynasties generally followed each other, except for the Abydos Dynasty which was not mentioned in Manetho's timeline. In the ULT, the Hyksos appear to have conquered the 14th Dynasty during a famine around 2533 BC. Seals from the 14th Dynasty have been found as far north as Tel Kabri, in modern-day Israel, and as far south as Dongola in modern-day Sudan,[13] indicating that the 14th Dynasty was still in control of the territory of the Middle Kingdom.

The Hyksos seized control of Egypt circa 2533 BC ULT, forming the 15th Dynasty, and in the process introduced the horse, the war-chariot, and compound bow to Egypt. This is itself an enigma, as in the CET the Hyksos invaded Egypt circa 1674 BC, introducing horses and war-chariots, almost a thousand years after they are known to have been in use in Sumer, as portrayed in the Standard of Ur from 2600 BC CMT. The Standard of Ur dates from the reign of King Ur-Pabilsag, who is not listed in the Sumerian King List, which would place his life sometime after the end of the Sumero-Akkadian Dynasty. He also is unknown from the later Old Babylonian, Old Assyrian, or Sealand King Lists, which would mean he must have existed somewhere during the Old Babylonian Dark Age between 3013 and 1373 BC ULT. This means that the Egyptians either lagged almost a thousand years behind the Sumerians technologically in the conventional timelines, or both cultures adopted the horse and chariot technology during the same dark age.

In the CET, the Hyksos 15th Dynasty was driven out of Egypt circa 1535 BC early in the 18th Dynasty,

---

[13] Kim Ryholt (1997) *The Political Situation in Egypt during the Second Intermediate Period*

after the rise and fall of the 16th, Abydos, and 17th Dynasties. In order for these dynasties to all coexist, they have to have only ruled specific regions. In the ULT, the Hyksos 15th Dynasty was driven out by the 16th Dynasty circa 2249 BC, which was an Egyptian-ized-Hyksos Dynasty based in Thebes, Egypt. In both timelines, the Abydos Dynasty rose up as a national-ist faction that fought a 70-year long war against the 15th or 16th Dynasty. In the CET, the Abydos Dy-nasty formed the 17th Dynasty circa 1580 BC and was replaced by the 18th Dynasty of the New King-dom in 1549 BC, who ultimately drove the Hyksos from Egypt circa 1535 BC. While in the ULT the Abydos Dynasty drove the 16th Dynasty from Egypt circa 1731 BC and then formed the 17th Dynasty which ruled until 1580 BC when the 18th Dynasty founded the New Kingdom. While we do have exten-sive records from the New Kingdom, there are no records of conflict with the Hyksos, the only existing record that Egyptologist use to date the war between the Hyksos and the 18th Dynasty is the military commentary on the back of the Rhind Mathematical Papyrus, consisting of brief diary entries, one of which reads:

> *"Regnal year 11, second month of shomu, Heli-opolis was entered. First month of akhet, day 23, this southern prince broke into Tjaru"*[14]

This diary entry does not state the name of either the ruling king or the rebel prince, and could just as easily be interpreted as the founder of the 18th Dy-nasty Prince Ahmose I's rebellion against his uncle

---

[14] Donald Redford (1992) *Egypt, Canaan, and Israel in Ancient Times*, Page 71

King Kamose of the 17th Dynasty. In fact, it makes far more sense that the writer would refer to the enemy as a prince if he was the nephew of the king, than if he was ruling a rebel faction. The fact that Heliopolis was invaded should point it not being a reference to the war against the Hyksos, as the Hyksos were based in Avaris in the Nile Delta, not Heliopolis in modern Greater Cairo.

It should also be noted that the Turin King List from the 19th Dynasty, less than 300 years later, does not record the 15th Dynasty Hyksos and 18th Dynasty coexisting, but rather it records the same thing that Manetho translated into Greek a thousand years later. The fact that the New Kingdom era Egyptians believed the 14th, 15th, 16th, 17th, and 18th Dynasties were sequential, spanning over 1200 years of history is well documented, yet ignored by Egyptologists. Egyptologists also choose to ignore the fact that both the 13th Dynasty (1803 to 1649 BC CET) and 16th Dynasty (1660 to 1600 BC CET), ruled from Thebes in overlapping concurrent dynasties. Two competing governments sharing a capital city for eleven years is a pretty abstract notion.

In the CET, when the Hyksos were driven out of Egypt around 1535 BC, they seem to have simply disappeared. While the Old Babylonian Empire had already been occupied by the Kassites and very little is known of the time in Babylonia, the Old Assyrian and Old Hittite Empires were still around, and neither recorded the army of 480,000 Hyksos that Manetho mentioned leaving Egypt. In the ULT, the Hyksos Dynasty was driven out of Egypt circa 2249 BC, deep into the Babylonian Dark Age, centuries after the collapse of the Old Assyrian and Old Hittite Empires.

As the Hyksos appear to have been mainly Semitic people, with a Hurrian nobility, they likely reintegrated into the Mitanni and Kassite Dynasty Babylonians. The last king of the Hyksos Dynasty was recorded by the Turin King List as Khamudi. His name had also been found on scarab seals in Jericho,[15] and a seal believed to be from Byblos has been discovered with the name Khondy on it,[16] which is generally believed to refer to Khamudi, although some Egyptologists believe it was a different, previously unknown Egyptian king.

The first Kassite king we know anything of was Agum II, also called Agum Kakrime, who is believed to have been the 8th or 9th king of the Third Babylonian Dynasty, meaning that there was an entire dynasty between the Old Babylonian Kingdom and the known Kassite Dynasty that we have no records of. Unfortunately, the oldest records of Agum II are from the Neo-Assyrian era around 700 years later, and therefore we cannot even know if this is accurate information. There are eight kings listed before Agum II on ancient Mesopotamian king lists, however, nothing is known of them, other than that the first three ruled for a combined length of 70 years.

The first Kassite King that can be synchronized with the king lists of another culture is Burnaburiash

---

[15] Darrell D. Baker (2008) *The Encyclopedia of the Pharaohs: Volume I - Predynastic to the Twentieth Dynasty 3300-1069 BC.* Page 174

[16] Flinders Petrie (1917) *Scarabs and cylinders with names: illustrated by the Egyptian collection in University College, London*

I, who concluded a treaty with the Assyrian King Puzur-Ashur III, sometime around 1580 BC. Burnaburiash I was the 10th king listed in the Kassite dynasty, and if the first three king's reigns, ranging from 22 to 26 years, are of similar length to the first seven king's reigns, then the Kassite dynasty should have started approximately 225 years before the reign of Burnaburiash I, or approximately 1800 BC ULT. According to the ancient *Mesopotamian King List A*, the Kassites ruled Babylonia for 576 years and 9 months, over the course of 36 kings. As the last king of the Kassite Dynasty was Enlil-nadin-ahi, whose reign ended in about 1155 BC, this would indicate the Kassite Dynasty began in 1731 BC. This year is the same year that the Egyptianized-Hyksos 16th Dynasty was driven from Egypt in the ULT. As the monarchs of the Egyptianized-Hyksos Dynasty would have been used to living in opulence, the most likely place for them to have traveled to with their army of 480,000, was Babylonia, which would explain the foundation of a new dynasty at this point in time.

Unfortunately, the conventional Mesopotamian timeline does not allow this, as Babylon wasn't sacked until 1595 BC, meaning the Kassite dynasty must date to after that. As a result, Assyriologists ignore the early Kassite kings, and the CMT only allows 350 years for the Kassite dynasty. After the Egyptians drove the Hyksos from Egypt, they launched several campaigns deep into Canaan, crossing into Mitanni territory. The Egyptian King Thutmose III launched an invasion of the Mitanni Empire around 1457 BC, after defeating the combined forces of the cities of Megiddo and Kadesh and their allies, including the 330 Mitanni tribal leaders. The invasion of the Mitanni Empire was ultimately a failure, and Egypt acquired no territory from the Mitanni, however, the token Mitanni militia encountered was defeated.

The Assyrian homeland had already regained its independence from the Mitanni before the Battle of Megiddo in 1457 BC, and would go on to restore the lost Assyrian Empire in the following centuries. The capital city of the Mitanni, Washukanni, was sacked by the Hittites under Suppiluliuma I, sometime around 1320 BC, and they installed the vassal King Shattiwaza. Shortly thereafter the Mitanni fell under the domination of the resurgent Assyrian Empire. Washukanni was sacked again around 1250 BC, this time by the Assyrians after a failed attempt by the Mitanni to succeed from the Assyrian Empire. In Babylonia, the Kassite dynasty fought a series of losing wars against the Assyrian Middle Kingdom until they ultimately fell to the Elamites of southern Iran circa 1155 BC.

The fact that the Egyptians could launch a major offensive into Canaan in 1457 BC, invading the Mitanni Empire, yet finding no trace of the Hyksos, just 80 years after they were driven out of Egypt in 1535 BC CET, points to the CET being fundamentally wrong. If the Hyksos were driven out of Egypt in 2249 BC ULT, almost 800 years before the Battle of Meggido, it would explain why there was no trace of them in 1457 BC. Egyptologists also dispute the length of the last king of the Hyksos reign, providing estimates of 1 to 12 years, however, do agree that

Khamudi was ultimately driven from Canaan.

For centuries historians have suggested that Khamudi may have been the legendary founder of the Greek city-state of Thebes: Cadmus (Κάδμος / Kadmos).[17] According to Herodotus, Cadmus lived sixteen hundred years before his time, which would mean he lived sometime before 2000 BC. The City of Thebes is believed to have been founded sometime during the Early Helladic III Period, between 2200 and 2000 BC. This generally corresponds to Khamudi leaving Egypt circa 2249 BC ULT, but cannot line up with Khamudi leaving Egypt circa 1535 BC CET. Cadmus was recorded by various ancient Greco-Roman sources as coming from Tyre,[18] Sidon,[19] or Egypt.[20] While the theory of Khamudi being Cadmus is far from generally accepted by Egyptologists, as Cadmus had to have founded Thebes in Greece long before Khamudi was driven from Egypt in the CET, this idea dates back to at least the time of ancient Rome, and is why Roman historian Diodorus Siculus recorded Cadmus originating in Egypt.

---

[17] David Rohl (2007) *Lords of Avaris*, Pages 494-6
[18] Herodotus (c. 450 BC) *Histories*, II, 49
[19] Euripides (c. 425 BC) *Bacchae*, 171
[20] Diodorus Siculus (c. 20 AD) *Bibliotheca Historica* I, 23

Dynastic Mesopotamia in the CMT

In the CMT, the Ubaid civilization existed from at least 8000 BC, based on the existence of bullae dating back to that period, which then evolved into Sumerian clay tablets, but somehow, the Sumerians knew nothing about them, and instead wrote elaborate nonsense about ancient Sumerian dynasties in the same cities and at the same time the Ubaidians were there. The Sumerian civilization then appeared fully formed building massive temple complexes identical to the Ubaidians, whom they didn't know anything about, around 2900 BC.

The Sumerian civilization was only around for a few hundred years, and then fell to the Akkadians around 2334 BC. The Akkadian civilization spanned Mesopotamia, and regional kingdoms rose to prominence in Assyria circa 1905 BC and Babylonia circa 1894 BC. The last of the Sumero-Akkadian dynasties fell to the Babylonians in 1788 BC, for no particular reason.

In approximately 1674 BC a group of Semites and Hurrians that appear to have been led by Mitanni, but weren't because there were no Mitanni yet, peacefully migrated into northern Egypt, and formed the Hyksos Dynasty. They appeared out of nowhere, which is convenient because when they were driven back out of Egypt around 1535 BC, they just vanished.

In 1595 BC, Babylon was destroyed by the Hittites, from Anatolia, and a couple of decades later the Kassites invaded and settled in Babylonia. They are believed to have been related to Hurrians, and had an Indo-European nobility, like the Mitanni. Immediately after the Hittites destroyed Babylon in 1595 BC, a group of Indo-Aryans seized control of the Hurrian population in modern Syria, and instantaneously formed the Mitanni Empire, driving back both the Hittite and Assyrian Empires. Around 1560 BC, during the reign of the Assyrian King Nur-ili, the Mitanni Empire sacked Ashur, capital of the Assyrian Empire, and shortly afterward the entire Assyrian Empire fell under the dominion of the Mitanni. This means that the Mitanni had less than 35 years to liberate the Hurrians from the Hittites and Assyrians, and conquer the Canaanites, before sacking Ashur.

Around 1457 BC the Egyptian King Thutmose III launched an invasion of the Mitanni empire in Syria, and met only token resistance from the local militia. By 1390 BC the Mitanni Empire was losing ground to the resurgent Hittite and Assyrian Empires, and circa 1340 BC the Hittites sacked the Mitanni capital Washukanni and installed a vassal king. In circa 1276 the Assyrians occupied Washukanni, and made the former Mitanni empire into part of their Middle Kingdom.

Dynastic Mesopotamia in the ULT

In the ULT, the Ubaid civilization was the Sumerian civilization, which existed from at least 8000 BC based on the existence of bullae dating back to that period, which then evolved into the Sumerian era clay tablets. The Sumerians did have records of that early time, which they recorded as the historic dynasties of Sumer.

The Sumerian civilization was around for thousands of years, before falling to the Akkadians around 3885 BC. The Akkadian civilization spanned Mesopotamia, and regional kingdoms rose to prominence in Assyria circa 3278 BC and Babylonia circa 3352 BC. The last of the Sumero-Akkadian dynasties fell to the Babylonians around 3227 BC, as a result of the Great Shock of 3250 BC when the southern marshlands of Mesopotamia would have been drowning under the extra rainwater.

In approximately 3038 BC, Babylon was destroyed by the Hittites, from Anatolia, and the region fell into chaos. This region was later colonized by a group of people called the Kassites, who were led by an Indo-Aryan nobility. These Indo-Aryans and Kassites backed an insurgent Hurrian uprising in Hittite and Assyrian lands, which then formed into the Mitanni Empire.

The Mitanni later conquered Egypt in circa 2533 BC forming the Hyksos 'foreign ruler' dynasty. The Hyksos rule was overthrown by an Egyptianized-Hyksos 16th Dynasty in 2249 BC which ruled from Thebes in southern Egypt. The Hyksos that were driven from Egypt around 2249 BC reintegrated with the Mitanni and Kassite population of Babylonia. The Egyptianized-Hyksos 16th Dynasty was later driven out of Egypt in 1731 BC and seized power in Babylonia forming the Third Babylonian Dynasty.

Around 1457 BC the Egyptian King Thutmose III launched an invasion of the Mitanni empire in Syria and met only token resistance from the local militia. By 1390 BC, the Mitanni Empire was losing ground to the resurgent Hittite and Assyrian Empires, and around 1340 BC the Hittites sacked the Mitanni capital Washukanni and installed a vassal king. In circa 1276 BC, the Assyrians occupied Washukanni, and made the former Mitanni empire into part of their Middle Kingdom. The Assyrians also conquered most of the Kassite ruled Babylonia, before it ultimately fell to the Elamites circa 1158 BC.

Part 2: Pre-Dynastic Mesopotamia

PRE-DYNASTIC MESOPOTAMIAN TIMELINE		
CIVILIZATION	**DYNASTY**	**ULT**
Eridug	Alulim	266,379 to 237,579 BC
Eridug	Alalngar	237,579 to 201,579 BC
Bad-tibira	En-men-lu-ana	201,579 to 158,379 BC
Bad-tibira	En-men-gal-ana	158,379 to 129,579 BC
Bad-tibira	Dumuzid	129,579 to 93,579 BC
Larag	En-sipad-zid-ana	93,579 to 64,779 BC
Zimbir	En-men-dur-ana	64,779 to 43,779 BC
Shuruppag	Ubara-Tutu	43,779 to 25,179 BC
Kish	1st Kish	25,179 to 7698 BC
Dynastic Era		9868 to 3227 BC

Like the Egyptians, the Sumerians recorded a long pre-dynastic history. The Sumerians recorded a series of king lists for different cities, which they claimed ruled Mesopotamia in sequence, with the kingship being taken from city to city. Modern Assyriologists generally disregard the idea that the kingship passed from city to city in a long line of dynasties, as this would push the foundation of Sumer back to approximately 23,645 BC, after the Flood of Ziusudra. Adding the dynasties listed before the flood, human history would have begun approximately 264,845 BC.

This is a tremendous period of time and is generally disregarded by both Assyriologists and historians as being nothing more than myths. However, humans were around at the time, and the brief records of the time-periods in question do correlate with significant events in human prehistory as determined by research into geology, paleoclimatology, and archaeogenetics.

Kish Civilization

1ST KISH DYNASTY TIMELINE	
KING	**ULT**
Jushur	25,179 to 23,979 BC
Kullassina-bel	23,979 to 23,019 BC
Nangishlishma	23,019 to 22,349 BC
En-tarah-ana	22,349 to 21,929 BC
Babum	21,929 to 21,629 BC
Puannum	21,629 to 20,789 BC
Kalibum	20,789 to 19,829 BC
Kalumum	19,829 to 18,989 BC
Zuqaqip	18,989 to 18,089 BC
Atab	18,089 to 17,489 BC
Mashda	17,489 to 16,649 BC
Arwium	16,649 to 15,929 BC
Etana	15,929 to 14,429 BC
Balih	14,429 to 14,029 BC
En-me-nuna	14,029 to 13,396 BC
Melem-Kish	13,396 to 12,469 BC
Barsal-nuna	12,469 to 11,269 BC
Zamug	11,269 to 11,129 BC
Tizqar	11,129 to 10,824 BC
Ilku	10,824 to 9924 BC
Ilta-sadum	9924 to 8724 BC
En-me-barage-si	8724 to 7824 BC
Aga	7924 to 7698 BC

The earliest kings whose names we have found on ancient artifacts, are Enmebaragesi and Aga, the last two kings of the 1st Kish Dynasty. According to the Epic of Gilgamesh King Enmebaragesi conquered Elam, in southern Iran, and then turned his eye towards Uruk. King Dumuzid, the fisherman, of Uruk ultimately conquered Kish, and then apparently forced the former King Enmebaragesi to live as a woman. As transgender men and women are documented as part of the Sumerian culture, it is unclear if this indicates that Enmebaragesi was a female living as a male while he was king, or if Dumuzid, the fisherman, was a sadist who forced the conquered male king to live as a woman.

Assyriologists generally accept that Enmebaragesi and Aga existed, along with Dumuzid and Gilgamesh, however, don't accept the earlier kings in the 1st Kish Dynasty. One of the issues of dating the 1st Kish Dynasty is that it is unclear if the different Kish Dynasties were located in the same City of Kish, or even in a city at all during the early era. The ruins of the City of Kish are believed to have been near Tell al-Uhaymir, close to the city of Babylon.

The unclear nature of the 1st Kish Dynasty has led to the proposal by the Assyriologist Ignace Gelb, that early Kish may have been a culture, and not a city. In Gelb's proposal, Kish was the original Semitic culture that the Akkadians and Amorites descended from. There is some evidence supporting this theory in the *Sumerian King List* itself, as many of the kings of the 1st Kish Dynasty do have Semitic names. Unfortunately, this cannot be seen as conclusive evidence for a Semitic dynasty as some of the names are Sumerian, and the oldest copies of the Sumerian King List date to the Akkadian era, and therefore the Semitic names could simply be translations of the original Sumerian names. There is some evidence that the Akkadians did translate parts of the king list into Akkadian, as the second name on the list, Kullassina-bel, translates as 'All of them (were) lord' in Akkadian. This is generally read as a sign that the period was either without government or was some kind of republic. The period of Kullassina-bel was recorded as being 960 years long.

If one accepts the premise of the ULT, that the Ubaid civilization was the Sumerian dynastic period, from the 1st Uruk Dynasty through the end of the 3rd Uruk Dynasty, when Sargon of Akkad seized control of Mesopotamia, circa 3885 BC ULT, then the Kish civilization would have happened between 25,179 and 7698 BC. This Kish civilization started in the aftermath of a great flood that was the precursor for the later story of Noah's flood from Jewish folklore, which then found its way into the Christian and Islamic religions.

It is a very strange time period for the ancient Sumerians to have stated there was a major flood, as it is at the approximate date that the ice-sheets reached their greatest extent during the last glacial maximum, which is estimated at 26,500 years ago. The lowest level that the ocean level reached during the last glacial maximum is estimated at 135 meters below the current sea level, sometime between 29,000 and 21,000 years ago.[21] After the ice-sheets

[21] Kurt Lambeck, et al. (October 28, 2014) "Sea level and global ice volumes from the Last Glacial Maximum to the Holocene,"

reached their peak, the ice-sheets began melting, and global coastlines began drowning as the ocean levels began to rise. The Sumerian King List places this date as about 25,179 BC.

After the flood of Ziusudra, the first king on the Sumerian King List was Jushur who rained for 1200 years. As the following 'king' was Kullassina-bel, whose name means 'All of them (were) lord,' which clearly isn't the name of a king, but rather the description of the time. This implies that Jushur and the rest of the long-lived 'kings' were in fact periods of time, or possibly dynasties or even civilizations. There is very little information that remains from the Kish civilization, the first 12 'kings' are completely unknown other than their mention in the Sumerian King List.

The 13th king, Etana, is known from later Babylonian and Assyrian stories about him. He was known as 'the shepherd, who ascended to heaven and consolidated all the foreign countries.' In the story of Etana, he became involved in a struggle between an anthropomorphize serpent, and an anthropomorphize eagle. The serpent-man mutilated a cow, and when the eagle-man came to investigate the carcass the serpent-man caught the eagle-man and locked him in a pit. Etana found the pit and freed the eagle-man, after which the eagle-man flew Etana up to heaven, where Etana found the cure for impotence. While this story is quite strange, it does seem to be a precursor to the war between the man-bird angels and the serpent-devil of the Judaeo-Christian reli-

Proceedings of the National Academy of Sciences, 111 (43) 15296-15303

gions. This time period of King Etana, between 15,941 and 14,441 BC ULT, is also interesting as it is roughly the same period as Manetho's 30 Kings of Memphis.

No other information about the Kish Dynasty survives until Enmebaragesi who was captured by Dumuzid the Fisherman circa 7836 BC ULT. Aga continued to rule Kish for some time after Enmebaragesi's capture, however, according to the king list, the kingship was transferred to Uruk, meaning Aga would have simply been a local governor. If the Kish culture was a Semitic culture, the transfer of the kingship to Uruk was the beginning of the Sumerian period.

Antediluvian Shuruppak

Before the beginning of the Kish civilization, the Sumerian King List claims that there was the Flood of Ziusudra. While this flood served as a forerunner for the Flood of Noah, it was not depicted as being a worldwide phenomenon the way the later Jewish story was. The early Jews most likely knew of the many flood stories from across their world and interpreted them as one world-wide flood. In fact, the coastal regions of the world have been flooding since the height of the glacial maximum during the last glacial period, sometime between 29,000 and 21,000 years ago.

The melting of the ice-sheets has not been consistent and has occasionally reversed, as the ice-sheets temporarily increased in mass during brief reversals. Nevertheless, the global ocean levels have been generally rising since the Last Glacial Maximum. This sea-level increase has generally been slow, however, has included rapid sea-level change periods, when large amounts of ice suddenly melted. Ice-core samples from Antarctica and Greenland, along with studies of a variety of submerged land features, have shown there has been a series of rapid ocean rise periods, called meltwater pulses. These meltwater pulses are known as MWP-1A0 around 19,000 years ago, MWP-1A between 14,700 to 13,500 years ago,[22] MWP-1B between 11,500 to 11,200 years ago,[23] and MWP-1C between 8200 and 7600 years ago.[24]

---

[22] Vivien Gornitz (2009) *Encyclopedia of paleoclimatology and ancient environments.* Page 890 (Table S1)

[23] T. M. Cronin (2012) "Rapid sea-level rise," *Quaternary Science Reviews,* 56:11-30

[24] P. Blanchon (2011) "Meltwater Pulses," *Encyclopedia of Mod-*

These meltwater pulses are no doubt the cause of many of the world's flood myths, and if the *Sumerian King List* is to be believed, the first one was circa 25,179 BC. There are several versions of Ziusudra's flood from throughout the history and cultures of Mesopotamia where he had several names. Ziusudra and Zin-Suddu were the names used by the Sumerians, Utnapishtim was his Akkadian name, and Atrahasis was later used by the Babylonians. None of these appear to be real names, Ziusudra translates as 'life of long days,' Utnapishtim translates as 'he who saw life,' and Atrahasis translates as 'exceedingly wise.' While it is possible that someone would name their child 'exceedingly wise,' the other names are clearly not proper names, and as the 'exceedingly wise' Atrahasis was the most recent name used by Mesopotamians, circa 1894 to 1595 BC CMT (3352 to 3038 BC ULT), it is clear that we don't know what his name actually was.

ern Coral Reefs: Structure, form and process. Springer-Verlag Earth Science Series, Page 683-690

Ziusudra, Utnapishtim, and Atrahasis

The stories of Ziusudra, Utnapishtim, and Atrahasis, are all essentially the same, although embedded in the larger narratives of their respective cultures. The *Epic of Atrahasis* from circa 3352 to 3038 BC ULT (1894 to 1595 BC CMT), was the most comprehensive. It began with the gods dividing control of the world between them, Anu getting control of the sky, Ellil getting control of the land, and Ea getting control of the water. This story is mirrored in many ancient mythologies, such as the Hurrian Anu-Kumarbi-Teshub triad, the Canaanite Hadad-Mot-Yamm triad, the Greek Zeus-Hades-Poseidon triad, and the Latin Jupiter-Orcus-Neptune triad. As all of these cultures rose to prominence after the time of the Old Babylonian Empire, the stories could have been copied from the Babylonians.

The *Epic of Atrahasis* continued with Ellil assigning a group of lesser gods to work as farmers and engineers, however, after working for some time they rebelled and refused to continue working for Ellil. Ea suggested that the gods create a new race to work as farmers and engineers, and so humans were made. Unfortunately, the humans bred rapidly, and the land became so overpopulated that Ellil decided to limit the human population by releasing plagues and famines every 1200 years, however, that was not enough to stop the human population growth, so Ellil decided to flood the land to wipe out humanity. Ea warned Atrahasis of the coming flood, and so Atrahasis pulled down his house and built a boat large enough for his family and friends to survive.

The river where Atrahasis lived then flooded, and Atrahasis and his family and friends survived. Like the earlier Sumerian and Akkadian versions of Atrahasis, he was identified as being the King of Shuruppak before the flood.

The earlier Akkadian version of the story is found embedded in the *Epic of Gilgamesh*. King Gilgamesh, bereaved by the death of his best friend Enkidu, set off to find the ancient survivor of the flood Utnapishtim. It is explained within the epic that Utnapishtim was awarded immortality after the flood, which is why he was still around thousands of years later. The flood is also described, generally similar to the later Epic of Atrahasis. In the Utnapishtim version, Ea appeared to Utnapishtim in a dream and told him to build a cube-shaped ship, 200 feet long, wide, and high. Inside this wooden building were seven stories, each divided into nine sections, where Utnapishtim's family, friends, workers, and some domesticated animals lived during the flood. In this version of the flood, the ship floated to the hills of northern Iraq, where Utnapishtim and his crew disembarked.

The earliest version of the story we have is found on a broken clay tablet recovered from the ruins of Nippur called the *Eridu Genesis*. In this version, the gods An, Enlil, Enki, and Ninhursanga created humans and made parts of the world safe to live in. Then the gods descended to Earth, and the first cities were built: Eridu, Bad-tibira, Larak, Zimbir, and Shuruppak. Later the gods decided to not save humanity from a coming flood, both the cause of the flood and the reason the gods would not help humanity are unknown due to damage to the tablet. Where the tablet's damage ends, Ziusudra is in a huge boat with his friends and family, and some livestock. After the flood An and Enlil award Ziusudra with immortality for saving mankind.

There is one significant difference between the story of Ziusudra and his Akkadian and Babylonian descendants. In Ziusudra's story, the city he lived in was not named Shuruppak, instead, Shuruppak was the name of the king. The *Eridu Genesis* tablet was found in the ruins of Nippur and dated to approximately 1600 BC CMT (2977 BC ULT). The dating itself is based on the debris the damaged tablet was found in, and it clearly dates to a much earlier time. 1600 BC CMT was the end of the Old Babylonian Empire, and the city of Nippur was neglected by the Old Babylonian Empire, as the religious focus of the empire had been turned to Babylon, and the supreme god of the Babylonians was Marduk, not Nippur's patron god Enlil. This broken tablet was clearly being thrown away in 1600 BC CMT, which is fortunate for us, as it is the only known copy of the Eridu Genesis to survive to the present.

As the text is written in Sumerian it is logical to assume it was written sometime during the Sumerian era. According to the ancient Sumerian *Tummal Chronicle*, the first king to build up the Temple of Enlil at Nippur was Enmebaragesi. Alabaster vase fragments bearing his name have been found at the ruins of Nippur, lending credence to this claim that he was involved in building the temple. Many other kings built up the Temple of Enlil over the rise and fall of dynasties, including Aga of Kish, Gilgamesh of Uruk, and Mesannepada of Ur.

The *Eridu Genesis* tablet was written in Sumerian cuneiform, and so the tablet must date to the Sumerian era, however, if the Sumerians were writing their pictographic script on papyrus before they started using clay tablets, then the story could be from any point in Sumerian history. This means that the *Eridu Genesis* could date from thousands of years before the dynastic city of Shuruppak was even founded.

Dynastic Shuruppak

The ruins of the dynastic city called Shuruppak are near modern Tel Fara, in southern Iraq. The city is believed to have been founded around 3100 BC CMT (or 4600 ULT), after a major river flood. Below the city's ruins are a layer of alluvium that has not been excavated, so, if the city was built on an older city that was flooded, we do not know. During its height, the dynastic city of Shuruppak was a major trading center, with more grain solos than any other known Sumerian city.

Assyriologists generally consider the story of antediluvian Shuruppak's flooding to relate to the layer of alluvium found under the city, meaning that the story of Ziusudra/Utnapishtim/Atrahasis' life can be dated to approximately 3100 BC CMT. While this is a convenient way to avoid having to deal with the idea that the flood happened at the height of the Last Glacial Maximum, it does seem to ignore the story of antediluvian Shuruppak being flooded, as the ruins of dynastic Shuruppak are built on top of the alluvium, not covered in it.

If the story of antediluvian Shuruppak's flooding is correct, then it is unlikely it will ever be found. If it was built near a coastal area, then it is under over 100 meters of water now, and if on a river mouth near a coast, probably under more than 25 meters of sediment. If it was along an inland river, it would be closer to the surface, but still buried for 25,000 years. Unless the ancient builders were building with materials that could have survived the elements for that long, there should be nothing left of it.

In the *Sumerian King List*, the city of Shuruppak was the fifth city built before the flood. This happened 18,600 years before Ziusudra's flood, approximately 45,800 years ago, after the city of Zimbir fell. The name Shuruppak means 'the healing place,' implying that the fall of Zimbir was traumatic, unfortunately, no information about this event survives. In the *Sumerian King List*, Ubara-Tutu is listed as the only king, having a reign of 18,600 years, however in the ancient Sumerian text The Instructions of Shuruppak, Shuruppak is listed as being Ubara-Tutu's heir, and Ziusudra is listed as being Shuruppak's heir, so Ubara-Tutu could not have been the only king. It seems likely given the names recorded in the following 1st Dynasty of Kish, that the Sumerians knew very little of the early times, and that no doubt included the antediluvian dynasties.

Shuruppaki Genetics

This time period is also interesting from a genetic perspective. Human mitochondrial DNA haplogroup-K is believed to have developed from haplogroup-U between 30,000 and 22,000 years ago, as the ocean levels were approaching their lowest level. This implies that during this time there was a significant population of mtDNA-HG-U people that settled somewhere, and some developed into mtDNA-HG-K people. This culture clearly had a large enough population that they could leave a significant genetic contribution to modern humanity. Haplogroup-K is found in approximately 10% of the native European population[25] and 6% of the Middle Eastern and North African population, with some groups having higher percentages, such as the Ashkenazi Jews at 32%,[26] Kurds at 17%,[27] French, Norwegians, and Bulgarians at 13.3%,[28] and Gurage of Ethiopia at 10%.[29]

Haplogroup-U did not disappear and continues to exist alongside haplogroup-K in Europe, the Middle East, and North Africa. The fact that haplogroup-U is also common in South Asia, while haplogroup-K is

[25] Bryan Sykes (2001) *The Seven Daughters of Eve*

[26] Doron M. Behar, et al. (May 2004) "MtDNA evidence for a genetic bottleneck in the early history of the Ashkenazi Jewish population," *European Journal of Human Genetics*, 12(5):355-64

[27] Lucia Simoni, et al. (2000) "Geographic Patterns of mtDNA Diversity in Europe," *American Journal of Human Genetics*, Volume 66, Pages. 262-278

[28] Vincent Dubut (2003) "mtDNA polymorphisms in five French groups: importance of regional sampling," *European Journal of Human Genetics*, 12: 293–300

[29] Amy Non (2010) *Analyses of genetic data within an interdisciplinary framework to investigate recent human evolutionary history and complex disease*

rare there, indicates that the culture that developed haplogroup-K was likely somewhere in the Middle East, North Africa, or Europe. This development of haplogroup-K from haplogroup-U circa 30,000 to 22,000 years ago, is undeniably at the same time as the Glacial Maximum of the last glacial period, circa 29,000 to 21,000 years ago. Given the global atmospheric dryness of the period, wherever this culture was, it was likely near a large body of water. This points to a coastal location on either the Arabian sea or Mediterranean coasts, approximately 130 meters below the modern sea level. Given the fact the haplogroup-K is common in Europe and North Africa, but rare in South Asia, the Mediterranean seems more likely than the Arabian Sea.

If one were considering the Mediterranean Sea, the Nile river also seems an obvious option. This time period is when the ancient Egyptians claimed there was an uninterrupted line of kings, from the time of Horus to King Bydis. This time period is the first one the Egyptians described as ruled by human kings and apparently existed between 30,435 and 16,535 years ago. As Bydis is believed to simply be the ancient Egyptian word for 'king,'[30] this clearly is only a very dimly-remembered time by dynastic Egypt, however, it was recorded as being in Egypt. As the Nile was even then the only major river emptying into the Eastern Mediterranean, it does seem likely that a culture would have settled in the ancient Nile delta. Unfortunately, that would leave the ruins of Shuruppak under 130 meters of water and

---

[30] W. G. Waddell, translator (1940) *Fragments of Manetho. Aegyptica Book 1*. Editor's Note 2.

alluvium that have accumulated in the past 25,000 years.

Antediluvian Zimbir

According to the Sumerian King List before the time of Shuruppak, the kingship was in Zimbir for 21,000 years. Meaning that Zimbir would have been founded approximately 64,800 years ago, after the city of Larak fell. Zimbir is the direct translation of the ancient Sumerian name, generally used by historians when dealing with the antediluvian city, however, Assyriologists prefer the Akkadian name Sippar when referring to the dynastic city. There were at least two cities called Sippar in dynastic Sumer: Sippar-Amnanum and Sippar-Yahrurum. Unfortunately, early archaeologists in the 1800s did not keep good records of where they excavated artifacts from and simply labeled items as coming from Sippar. This has resulted in some confusion over which Sippar ancient tablets came from, Sippar-Yahrurum or Sippar-Amnanum.[31] Sippar-Yahrurum was the larger of the two, said to have been founded by Ziusudra after the flood to serve as a library. The classical Babylonian historian Berossus claimed Ziusudra buried the records of the world from before the flood at Sippur-Amnanum.[32] Clearly, this Sippur was not the Zimbir that would have been destroyed around 45,800 years ago.

The ruins of Sippar-Yahrurum are found at Tel Abu Habbah near Yusufiyah, in central Iraq. Sippar-Yahrurum is known to have been occupied since at least the Early Uruk period, which would fall between 9900 and 7500 BC ULT (4000 to 3100 BC

---

[31] Anne Goddeeris (2002) *Economy and Society in Northern Babylonia in the Early Old Babylonian Period*

[32] Archibald Henry Sayce (1911) "Sippara," *Encyclopædia Britannica*, 25, 11th Edition, Page 151

CMT). In either timeline the city of Sippar-Yahrurum predates the flooding of dynastic Shuruppak, meaning that this city could not have been founded after the flooding of dynastic Shuruppak by Ziusudra. This supports the idea that dynastic Shuruppak was not the city that was flooded during Ziusudra's life.

The name Zimbir is believed to be the source of the Sumerian word 'sipru' which means writing. The implication is that the Sumerians either invented or originally taught writing in the city of Sippar-Yahrurum. The city of Sippar is one of the known sources for ancient waxed wooden writing boards, that were used as early as the Late Uruk period, circa 5231 to 4931 BC ULT, (3400 to 3100 BC CMT). These writing boards were used for a wide range of purposes, from training scribes in cuneiform, to administering the city. It appears that they may have been the major form of record-keeping during later periods of Sumerian history,[33] unfortunately, few have survived from the Sumerian era.

The name Zimbir itself is believed to translate as 'bird city' in Sumerian,[34] which when combined with being the root of the word for writing, forces us to consider the possibility that carrier pigeons could have originated at Zimbir. It is known that the Mesopotamians were using carrier birds of some kind by the time of Sargon circa 3885 to 3845 BC

---

[33] John MacGinnis (2002) "The use of writing boards in the Neo-Babylonian temple administration at Sippar," *Iraq*, 64, 217-236
[34] Maximillien de Lafayette (2017) "Vol.1. Etymology, Philology And Comparative Dictionary Of Synonyms," *22 Dead And Ancient Languages*, Page 79

ULT (2334 to 2299 BC CMT), called the ʻiṣ-ṣur-tú.'[35] Carrier pigeons were used for carrying messages between cities and even countries in ancient times. They were still in use by western militaries through World War 2 and reported to be in use by the Islamic State as recently as 2016. It is believed that the ancient Egyptians were using carrier pigeons by the end of the 1st Dynasty circa 5510 to 5247 BC ULT (3100 to 2890 BC CET).[36]

---

[35] Manfried Dietrich (2003) *The Babylonian Correspondence of Sargon and Sennacherib*
[36] David Woods (1965) *A history of tactical communications techniques*

Axis-Mundi

According to the Sumerian King Lists, the king of Zimbir was Enmendurana. His name is generally translated as 'chief of the powers of Duranki.' Duranki translates as approximately 'the meeting-place of heaven and earth.'[37] This means that Enmendurana's name translates as approximately 'chief of the powers of the meeting-place of heaven and earth.' However, the Sumerian word 'en' was also used in archaic Sumerian to mean 'time' or 'era.' Meaning that Enmendurana can also be translated as 'time of the meeting-place of heaven and earth.' Whatever this is supposed to mean, it is clearly a description of a time period, and not a proper name, much like the later names of kings during the 1st Kish Dynasty.

This concept of the meeting-place of Heaven and Earth is known throughout many ancient cultures, generally referred to as the axis-mundi by academics. Many ancient cultures claimed that specific mountains were the axis-mundi, such as the Canaanites, who claimed Mount Hermon was the axis-mundi. In the ancient Jewish *Book of the Watchers*, the Watchers first descended to Earth on Mount Hermon, which is possibly descended from an earlier Canaanite story.[38] In the Jewish religion, Mount Zion is the axis-mundi, the hill that Jerusalem is built on. In Christianity the axis-mundi is not currently on Earth, it is God's City, which will eventually land on

---

[37] Andrew R. George (1992) "Babylonian topographical texts," *Orientalia Lovaniensia Analecta*, 40, xviii, Page 261

[38] Kelley Coblentz Bautch (25 September 2003) *A Study of the Geography of 1 Enoch 17-19: "no One Has Seen what I Have Seen."* pages 62–.

Mount Zion becoming the New Jerusalem.[39] The ancient Armenians believed that the gods had once lived on Mount Ararat, much as the ancient Greeks believed the gods lived on Mount Olympus. In traditional Chinese beliefs, the Kunlun Mountains were the axis-mundi, where the peach-tree of immortality could be found.[40]

In Hindu, Jain, and Buddhist beliefs the name of the mountain is Meru. Meru is a mythical mountain, which has been identified with several actual mountains, including the Pamir Mountains of Kashmir,[41] Mount Kailash in Tibet,[42] and Mount Sumeru in Java. The fact that Mount Meru has been identified as several modern mountains clearly points to the fact that the original location is lost. In the ancient Zoroastrian holy book the Avesta, the axis-mundi was the Hara Berezaiti, which translates as High Watchpost. This mountain was surrounded by the steppes of the Aryan ancestral homeland, Airyanem Vaejah. The Airyanem Vaejah is described as being in the Arctic, before the beginning of the last glacial period, which if interpreted literally would be the Byrranga Mountains on the Taymyr Peninsula in Siberia. This name 'High Watchpost' has an odd similarity to the early-Jewish story of the Watchers descending on Mount Hermon, indicating that the Persian-era Jews may have been partially inspired by the Avestan story,

---

[39] Revelation of John 21:1-4
[40] Lihui Yang (2005) *Handbook of Chinese Mythology*. Pages 160-164
[41] George Nathaniel Curzon (1968) *The Hindu World: An Encyclopedic Survey of Hinduism*, Page 184
[42] Robert E. Buswell (2004) *Encyclopedia of Buddhism: A-L.* Pages 407-408

merging it with the ancient Canaanite story, as they appear to have merged several flood narratives.

There is an old Akkadian story of Enmendurana, where he is called Emmeduranki, that seems like a half-way point between the ancient Sumerian story of Enmendurana, and the Jewish story of Enoch and the Watchers. In the story, Emmeduranki was taken to heaven by the gods Utu and Adad, where he was taught the secrets of heaven and earth,[43] much as Enoch was in the Book of the Watchers.[44] Additionally, both Enoch and Enmendurana are the seventh antediluvian monarchs/patriarchs in their respective cultures.[45]

The Akkadians had their own version of the axis-mundi, Mount Mashu, which Gilgamesh had to pass through to get to the Garden-of-the-Gods on his way to meet Utnapishtim. Mount Mashu's location is also unknown, it was described as being a long way to the east of Uruk. These axis-mundi mountains are found in diverse cultures throughout the world, and in countries without mountains, people for some reason built them and then treated them as the axis-mundi. This was the case for the Giza pyramids in Egypt, the E-anna Ziggurat in Uruk, and the pyramids of Teotihuacán in Mexico. This concept of axis-mundi is clearly very old, with many specific points across Eurasia and North Africa being identified as

[43] Wilfred G. Lambert (1967) "Enmeduranki and Related Material," *Journal of Cuneiform Studies.* Vol. 21, Special Volume Honoring Professor Albrecht Goetze, pages 126-138

[44] J. J. Collins (1998) *The apocalyptic imagination: an introduction to Jewish apocalyptic literature.* Pages 44-47

[45] Victor Hamilton (1990) "The Book of Genesis" *The New International Commentary on the Old Testament.* Pages 257-258

being the axis-mundi, along with some in the Americas. This means that the idea must date back to a very early point in human pre-history before humanity settled in the Americas. The settlement of the Americas is a topic that causes a great deal of debate, however, remains of a settlement at Monte Verde in Chile have been carbon-dated to 33,000 years ago,[46] meaning that the concept of the axis-mundi is likely older than that.

The axis-mundi was not always a mountain, it was also commonly depicted as a tree in Eurasian cultures, such as the German Yggdrasil, Baltic Austras koks, Hungarian Égig érő fa, Turkic Ağaç Ana, Mongolian Modun, and Chinese Jianmu. The Ashvattha from the Vedic texts of ancient India is interpreted by many as an axis-mundi.[47] World-trees are a common element of Native American beliefs, found depicted in Aztec, Izapan, Mayan, Mixtec, and Olmec architecture. In the ancient Mayan Book of Chilam Balam, the world-tree was called the *Yax imix che*.[48] The fact that world-tree axis mundi is generally found in the cultures of the Eurasian Plains or those that had long contact with them, as well as the native American cultures points to the origin of the world-tree axis-mundi as a story these cultures once shared, presumably before they migrated away from a common area. These tree axis-mundis also have counterparts in many of the mountain axis-mundis. In ancient Chinese folk religion, the Peach Tree of Immortality was located in the

---

[46] Mark Rose (September 3, 1998) *Archaeology Magazine*

[47] *Rig Veda*, Book 4, Hymn 47, Verse 24

[48] Ralph L. Roys (1967) *The Book of Chilam Balam of Chumayel.* Page 100

Kunlun Mountains. In the Sumerian religion on top of Mount Kur, was the Garden-of-the-Gods, where the Good Tree was located. This has been interpreted as a forerunner of the Jewish Tree of Knowledge in the Garden of Eden, which has also been interpreted as an axis-mundi.

Laschamp Event

Whatever the original axis-mundi event, the Sumerian King List places it between 64,779 and 43,779 years ago, which is odd timing if purely fictitious, as many Assyriologists would claim. The end of this time period correlates with the beginning of the Laschamp event, which was a short reversal of the Earth's magnetic field. The Laschamp event is estimated to have taken place between 43,400 to 39,400 years ago. During this time, magnetic north became astronomical south, and magnetic south became astronomical north. If anyone was watching the skies and looking at a compass the world would have seemed upside down. The reversed magnetic field lasted for about 440 years, with a 250-year transition to and from the upside-down world. The reversed field was 75% weaker than the normal field strength of the Earth's magnetic field. The increased amount of radiation reaching the surface of the Earth caused increased production of beryllium 10 and higher levels of carbon 14.[49] This event was first recognized in the late 1960s, as a geomagnetic reversal in the Laschamp lava flows of Clermont-Ferrand, France,[50] since then the magnetic excursion has been found in geological records from many parts of the world.

The cause of the Laschamp event is unknown. The fact that it happened at the time when the Sumerians

---

[49] N. R. Nowaczyk et al. (2012) "Dynamics of the Laschamp geomagnetic excursion from Black Sea sediments," *Earth and Planetary Science Letters*, Volume 351-352, Pages 54-69

[50] N. Bonhommet and J. Zähringer (1969) "Paleomagnetism and potassium argon age determinations of the Laschamp geomagnetic polarity event," *Earth and Planetary Science Letters*, Volume 6, Pages 43-4

claim Zimbir fell, could be incidental, however, it is difficult to explain why they would name the king as Enmendurana, the 'time of the axis-mundi,' and claim he was taught the secrets of heaven by Utu, the sun,[51] and Adad, the storm god,[52] implying a stormy time when there was a problem with the sun. If Zimbir did in fact use carrier pigeons, the reversed magnetic field would have also wreaked havoc with the bird's navigation, and likely caused the failure of the civilization's communication network.

The end of this era, when Zimbir fell, is not just the time of the Laschamp Event, it is also the time of very cold periods that seem to match the beginning and end of the Laschamp Event. These very cold and very dry periods happened between approximately 44,300 to 43,300 years ago, and 40,800 to 40,000 years ago.[53] They have been detected in both ice-core samples from Greenland, and the study of carbon isotopes from caves in Europe. During this time in Eastern Europe, the average temperature is believed to have dropped to subzero year-round, and permafrost spread down from the Scandinavian glaciers. This period of increased European permafrost is believed to have contributed to the downfall of the European neanderthals.[54] The combination of the sudden onset

[51] Jeremy Black and Anthony Green (1992) *Gods, Demons and Symbols of Ancient Mesopotamia: An Illustrated Dictionary*, Page 180-187

[52] Alberto R. W. Green (2003) *The Storm-God in the Ancient Near East*

[53] Michael Staubwasser, et al. (September 11, 2018) "Impact of climate change on the transition of Neanderthals to modern humans in Europe," *Proceedings of the National Academy of Sciences.* 115 (37) 9116-9121

[54] Jason Daley (August 29, 2018) "Climate Change Likely Iced

of this cold period, combined with the magnetic re-versal and weakened geomagnetic field of the Laschamp event, would have been traumatic to any culture at the time. The fact that modern-humans be-gan to migrate into neanderthal territory at this time, both in Europe and Siberia, does indicate that something major had changed within modern-human culture.

Neanderthals Out Of Existence"

Zimbari Genetics

The time period when Zimbir fell is also notable in terms of human archaeogenetics. Human mitochondrial DNA haplogroup-U is believed to have developed from haplogroup-R between 49,800 and 43,200 years ago.[55] This haplogroup is widespread, and found in the indigenous populations of Europe, the Middle East, South Asia, North Africa, and the Horn of Africa. It diverged into nine subclades as the populations separated from their common source, which seems to be Zimbir. The oldest known sample of haplogroup-U mtDNA was recovered from a Siberian skeleton dated to circa 45,000 years ago.[56] Archaeogenetic studies have found haplogroup-U mtDNA in the remains of dynastic Egyptians, the remains of the indigenous Guanche people of the Canary Islands,[57] and the remains of ancient Europeans. Today this haplogroup is found in between 8% and 15% of Indians,[58] and 11% of the native population of Europe.[59] The highest percentage are found in the Berbers at 29% and the Copts at 27.6%. Given that these are the two known descendants of the na-

---

[55] D. M. Behar, et al. (April 2012) "A "Copernican" reassessment of the human mitochondrial DNA tree from its root," *American Journal of Human Genetics*. 90 (4): 675-84

[56] J. M. Larruga, et al. (May 2017) "Carriers of mitochondrial DNA macrohaplogroup R colonized Eurasia and Australasia from a southeast Asia core area," *BMC Evolutionary Biology*. 17 (1): 115

[57] R. Rodríguez-Varela, et al. (November 2017) "Genomic Analyses of Pre-European Conquest Human Remains from the Canary Islands Reveal Close Affinity to Modern North Africans," *Current Biology*. 27 (21): 3396–3402.e5

[58] M. Karmin (2005) "Human mitochondrial DNA haplogroup R in India," University of Tartu.

[59] B. Sykes (2001) *The Seven Daughters of Eve*

tive North African populations, it is plausible that Zimbir could have been in North Africa.

In order for this haplogroup to have developed, there would have needed to be a significant number of mtDNA-HG-R people, within which the mtDNA-HG-U group developed between 49,800 and 43,200 years ago. This new Zimbiri population would later found the Shuruppaki population, perhaps in the ancient Nile delta. The location of Zimbir itself was logically somewhere in the region where haplogroup-U is found today, Europe, the Middle East, North Africa, or South Asia, although Europe should be excluded as a potential location, as it was inhabited by Neanderthals at the time, and modern humans only began entering the region between 45,000 and 43,000 years ago, around the time Zimbir fell. The source of haplogroup-U is generally assumed to be somewhere in the Middle East, Anatolia, or the Caucasus Mountains.

Antediluvian Larak

In the Sumerian King List, before the kingship was in Zimbir, it was in the city of Larak, which fell approximately 64,800 years ago, after being around for 28,800 years, meaning it was founded circa 93,600 years ago. So far, no ruins have been found in Iraq associated with a dynastic city called Larak, however, it is believed they may lie somewhere near the ruins if Isin. Almost nothing is known about Larak. The King of Larak was said to be En-Sipadzidana of which there are no surviving stories. The name En-Sipadzidana translates approximately as 'time of the shepherd for the faithful of heaven,' which doesn't really enlighten us as to what Larak was, other than that they were apparently shepherding.

Sheep are believed to have been domesticated in the Middle East, approximately 13,000 years ago[60], however, the wild mouflon species which sheep were domesticated from, have been around for approximately four million years,[61] and therefore sheep could have been domesticated earlier than 13,000 years ago. In fact, some studies have suggested that sheep may have been domesticated up to three times from three different wild mouflon species. Of course, the term shepherd could have been used metaphorically, as it is being used within the concept 'shepherd for the faithful of heaven,' which sounds like something a Christian minister might describe himself as being.

---

[60] Robert E. Krebs and Carolyn A. Krebs (2003) *Groundbreaking Scientific Experiments, Inventions & Discoveries of the Ancient World*

[61] BGI Shenzhen (June 5, 2014) "The Sheep Genome: Study shows how sheep first separated from goats," phys.org

The world was different between 94,000 and 65,000 years ago, and modern-humans weren't the only people on it. The Neanderthals and Denisovans of Eurasia were the other humans on the planet at the time. Modern-humans are believed to have initially left Africa sometime between 110,000 and 95,000 years ago,[62] and by 100,000 years ago humans and Neanderthals had begun interbreeding.[63] While modern-human remains are found in the Middle East earlier than 80,000 years ago, after 80,000 years ago they were replaced by Neanderthals. It is believed that modern-humans left the region because the world was cooling, which allowed the neanderthals to migrate down into the area from Eastern Europe or Central Asia. Somewhere in Eurasia, a group of modern-humans with some Neanderthal DNA did survive,[64] presumably in South Asia.[65] Between 55,000 and 45,000 years ago these modern-humans returned to the Middle East, as the neanderthals withdrew to Europe and Siberia.

If Larak existed between 94,000 to 65,000 years ago, and if its inhabitants were modern-humans,

[62] Rachel Lentz (September 22, 2016) "Past climate swings orchestrated early human migration waves out of Africa," phys.org

[63] Martin Kuhlwilm, et al (25 February 2016) "Ancient gene flow from early modern humans into Eastern Neanderthals," *Nature.* 530, Pages 429-33

[64] S. Sankararaman, et al. (2014) "The landscape of Neandertal ancestry in present-day humans," *Nature.* 507 (7492) Pages 354-57

[65] Mait Metspalu, et al. (August 2004) "Most of the extant mtDNA boundaries in south and southwest Asia were likely shaped during the initial settlement of Eurasia by anatomically modern humans," *BMC Genetics.* 5: 26

then it could not have existed in the Middle East. Based on the archaeogenetic evidence most likely regions for this culture would have been South Asia,[66] or Southeast Asia.[67] This early shepherding civilization of Larak would have suffered a near extinction-level set-back when the Toba Volcano exploded in Indonesia around 75,000 years ago. This volcanic super-eruption is estimated to have ejected so much ash and poisonous gasses into the atmosphere that it is believed to have caused a volcanic winter that would have lasted for up to ten years.[68] In India, the ash-fall left a layer 15 cm thick.[69] Until recent genetic research confirmed that the early Eurasian population had survived, it was believed that they had been wiped out by the Toba super-eruption.

---

[66] Suvendu Maji, et al. (2008) "Distribution of Mitochondrial DNA Macrohaplogroup N in India with Special Reference to Haplogroup R and its Sub-Haplogroup U," *International Journal of Human Genetics.* 8 (1-2): 85-96

[67] Jose M Larruga (23 May 2017) "Carriers of mitochondrial DNA macrohaplogroup R colonized Eurasia and Australasia from a southeast Asia core area." *BMC Evolutionary Biology.* 17

[68] A. Robock, et al. (2009) "Did the Toba Volcanic Eruption of ~74k BP Produce Widespread Glaciation?" *Journal of Geophysical Research.* 114: D10107

[69] S. C. Jones (2007) "The Toba Supervolcanic Eruption: Tephra-Fall Deposits in India and Paleoanthropological Implications," *The Evolution and History of Human Populations in South Asia.* Page 173-200

Laraki Genetics

As is the case for the later Zimbir and Shuruppak civilizations, archaeogenetics has identified a mitochondrial DNA haplogroup that is believed to have arisen during this time, haplogroup-R. This haplogroup is the direct ancestor of haplogroup-U, which arose during the late Zimbir period, which was the direct ancestor of haplogroup-K, which arose during the late Shuruppak period. There were other mitochondrial subclades around, R gave rise to B, F, R0, and pre-JT, other than U, however, these groups arose at different times. The Sumerian King List points to specific periods in time when apparently significant civilizations existed, and these points in time follow a specific human lineage, back through K to U to R.

Haplogroup-R is believed to have arisen around 66,000 years ago,[70] in either South Asia,[71] or Southeast Asia.[72] Haplogroup-R gave rise to several haplogroups: B, F, R0, pre-JT, and of course U, meaning that haplogroup-R and its descendants are spread over a vast swath of the world. Haplogroup-R and its descendants a found among the native populations of the Americas, Australia, Central Asia, Europe, the

[70] Pedro Soares (2009) "Correcting for Purifying Selection: An Improved Human Mitochondrial Molecular Clock," *The American Journal of Human Genetics.* 84 (6): 740-59

[71] S. C. Jones (2007) "The Toba Supervolcanic Eruption: Tephra-Fall Deposits in India and Paleoanthropological Implications," *The Evolution and History of Human Populations in South Asia.* Page 173-200

[72] S. C. Jones (2007) "The Toba Supervolcanic Eruption: Tephra-Fall Deposits in India and Paleoanthropological Implications," *The Evolution and History of Human Populations in South Asia.* Page 173-200

Horn of Africa, North Africa, the Pacific Islands, Papua, South Asia, and Southeast Asia. In fact, the only region where haplogroup-R and its descendants are rare is Sub-Saharan Africa. This has led to the logical conclusion that it originates in Asia.

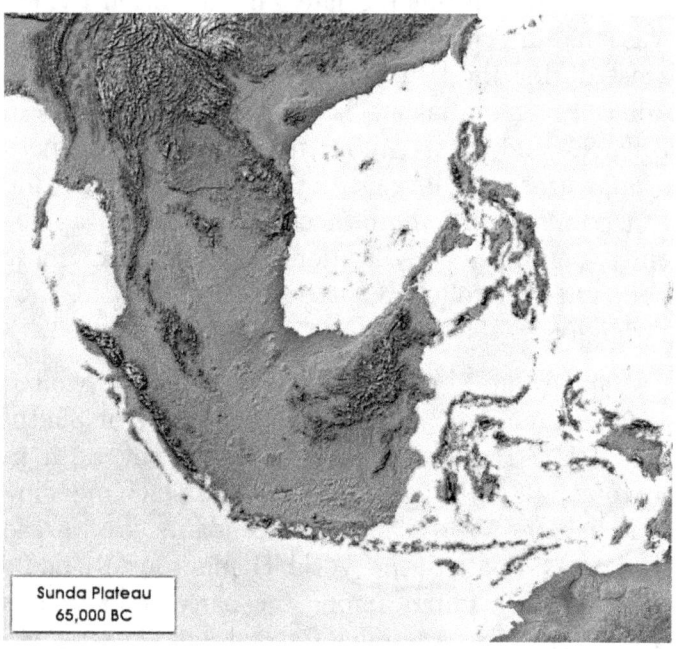

Sunda Plateau
65,000 BC

These early Laraki people colonized South Asia, the Southeast Asian Sunda Plateau, and the continent of Sahul (Australia and Papua) by 65,000 years ago.[73] Along the way, they encountered the Denisovans, who they interbred with. They could not have reached Sahul without boats of some kind, meaning

[73] Chris Clarkson, et al. (2017) "Human occupation of northern Australia by 65,000 years ago," *Nature.* 547 (7663): 306-310

that the Larak culture had to have been sea-faring. Given the high percentage of Denisovan DNA found in Papuans and Melanesians, it has been proposed that the Denisovans had also crossed to Sahul, where the primary interbreeding took place.[74] This would mean that the Denisovans were also seafaring, however, it is also possible that the two groups crossed to Sahul together after making contact on the Sunda Plateau. Based on the subclades that developed within the R haplogroup, it is possible to trace the migrations of peoples out of Larak.

Haplogroup-R0a is mostly found in the Middle East, North Africa, the Horn of Africa, and Central Asia. The highest percentage is found on the island of Socotra in the Arabian Sea, at 40%.[75] This suggests that this haplogroup may have originated in the now-submerged continental shelf of Arabia or East Africa.

Haplogroup-HV and its subclades are mainly found in Europe, the Middle East, Central Asia, South Asia, and North Africa. It is believed to have originated around 24,000 years ago in Anatolia or Caucasia.[76] The H subclade is the most common in Europe and is believed to have developed around 20,000 years ago in Southwest Asia.[77] The V subclade

---

[74] A. Cooper and C. B. Stringer (2013) "Did the Denisovans Cross Wallace's Line?" *Science.* 342 (6156): 321-23

[75] Amy Non (2010) *Analyses of genetic data within an interdisciplinary framework to investigate recent human evolutionary history and complex disease*

[76] B. Malyarchuk, et al. (2008) "Mitochondrial DNA Phylogeny in Eastern and Western Slavs," *Molecular Biology and Evolution.* 25 (8): 1651-8

[77] A. Achilli, et al. (November 2004) "The molecular dissection

is found at low frequencies throughout Europe, its highest percentage is found among the Sami people of Northern Europe, at 40%.[78]

Haplogroup-R1 and its descendants are mainly found in the Caucasian Mountains, with traces found in the Slavic populations to the north,[79] and the Brahmins of Uttar Pradesh[80] in India. This haplogroup is sometimes used as evidence that the Indo-Aryans originated on the Pontic Steppes north of Caucasia. R1's subclades R1a and R1b are also found in a high percentage in the indigenous population of the North American great lakes regions, and smaller percentages in Siberia and among the Fulani tribes of West Africa, although the cause for this wide distribution remains controversial.

Haplogroup-R2 is mainly found in Balochistan,[81] Pakistan, with smaller percentages across Rajasthan

---

of mtDNA haplogroup H confirms that the Franco-Cantabrian glacial refuge was a major source for the European gene pool," *American Journal of Human Genetics*. 75 (5): 910-8

[78] Agnar Helgason, et al. (2001) "MtDNA and the Islands of the North Atlantic: Estimating the Proportions of Norse and Gaelic Ancestry," *The American Journal of Human Genetics*. 68 (3): 723-37

[79] B. Malyarchuk, et al. (2008) "Mitochondrial DNA Phylogeny in Eastern and Western Slavs," *Molecular Biology and Evolution*. 25 (8): 1651-8

[80] Malliya Gounder Palanichamy, et al. (2004) "Phylogeny of Mitochondrial DNA Macrohaplogroup N in India, Based on Complete Sequencing: Implications for the Peopling of South Asia," *The American Journal of Human Genetics*. 75 (6): 966-78.

[81] Lluís Quintana-Murci, et al. (2004) "Where West Meets East: The Complex mtDNA Landscape of the Southwest and Central Asian Corridor," *The American Journal of Human Genetics*. 74 (5): 827-45

and Uttar Pradesh in India, and Iran, Turkey, and Georgia. If Balochistan was the location of the founder population, they may have been related to the Harappans or Elamites.

Haplogroup-J is mainly found in the Middle East, with the highest percentage found in Saudi Arabia at 21%.[82] Approximately 10% of Europeans, 8% of Caucasians, and 6% of North Africans carry mitochondrial DNA from this haplogroup. It is also believed to date from around 45,000 years ago, like U, and is almost nonexistent in East Asia, indicating the strong possibility that both originated in Zimbir.

Haplogroup-T is mainly found in the region around the Caspian Sea, in the Caucasus Mountains, Northern Iran, and Turkmenistan.[83] It is found in almost 10% of the European populations, with smaller percentages across the Middle East, Central Asia, South Asia, North Africa, and the Horn of Africa. It is believed to have developed in Anatolia sometime around 25,000 years ago.

Haplogroup-R3 is a rare haplogroup found in Armenia.

Haplogroup-R5 is widely spread across South Asia but is focused in Madhya Pradesh, India, at 17%,[84] indicating a possible location for the founder

---

[82] Khaled K. Abu-Amero, et al. (2008) "Mitochondrial DNA structure in the Arabian Peninsula," *BMC Evolutionary Biology.* 8: 45.

[83] Lluís Quintana-Murci, et al. (2004) "Where West Meets East: The Complex mtDNA Landscape of the Southwest and Central Asian Corridor," *The American Journal of Human Genetics.* 74 (5): 827-45

[84] Mait Metspalu, et al. (August 2004) "Most of the extant

population.

Haplogroup-R6 is a rare haplogroup found in South Asia, mainly in the Tamil and Kashmiri populations.[85]

Haplogroup-R7 is primarily found in eastern India, among Austroasiatic and Dravidian speaking populations.[86] Among the Austronesian speaking people of India, this haplogroup represents 10% of the population.

Haplogroup-R8 is mainly found in eastern India, mainly in Orissa, in Andhra Pradesh. It is also found in Gujarat. In Orissa, it represents 12% of the population and is focused in the Austroasiatic speaking population.[87] Orissa may have been the location of the founder population.

Haplogroup-R9 (R9b, R9c) is mainly found in Southeast Asia, throughout Indonesia, Malaysia, and Vietnam. The Batak people of the Philippines may have the highest percentage of R9 mitochondrial DNA at 58%.[88]

---

mtDNA boundaries in south and southwest Asia were likely shaped during the initial settlement of Eurasia by anatomically modern humans," *BMC Genetics.* 5: 26

[85] Mait Metspalu, et al. (August 2004) "Most of the extant mtDNA boundaries in south and southwest Asia were likely shaped during the initial settlement of Eurasia by anatomically modern humans," *BMC Genetics.* 5: 26

[86] Gyaneshwer Chaubey, et al. (2008) "Phylogeography of mtDNA haplogroup R7 in the Indian peninsula," *BMC Evolutionary Biology.* 8: 227

[87] Kumarasamy Thangaraj, et al. (2009) "Deep Rooting In-Situ Expansion of mtDNA Haplogroup R8 in South Asia," *PLoS ONE.* 4 (8): e6545

[88] Clarissa Scholes, et al. (2011) "Genetic diversity and evidence

<u>Haplogroup-F</u> is a major subclade of R9 spread across East and Southeast Asia. It is found in the populations of China, Indonesia, Thailand, and Vietnam. The highest percentages are found in remote regions around the periphery of East Asia, with 50% reported in the Nicobar Islands,[89] and 44% in the Shor people of Siberia.[90] This haplogroup is believed to have developed circa 43,400 years ago, somewhere in Asia.[91] As this haplogroup is not found in Native American populations, it likely developed in Southeast Asia. The collapse of this civilization may have been caused by the same climatic events that caused the collapse of Zimbir.

<u>Haplogroup-R11</u> is found in Cambodia, China, Japan, Laos, Thailand, and Vietnam, as well as Rajasthan, India. The largest concentrations seem to be in Yunnan, China, at 12.5%.[92]

<u>Haplogroup-B</u> is a common haplogroup among East Asian, Southeast Asian, Siberian, Oceanic, and Native American populations. This haplogroup is be-

---

for population admixture in Batak Negritos from Palawan," *American Journal of Physical Anthropology.* 146 (1): 62-72.

[89] Mait Metspalu, et al. (August 2004) "Most of the extant mtDNA boundaries in south and southwest Asia were likely shaped during the initial settlement of Eurasia by anatomically modern humans," *BMC Genetics.* 5: 26

[90] Miroslava Derenko, et al. (2007) "Phylogeographic Analysis of Mitochondrial DNA in Northern Asian Populations," *The American Journal of Human Genetics.* 81 (5): 1025-41

[91] Pedro Soares (2009) "Correcting for Purifying Selection: An Improved Human Mitochondrial Molecular Clock," *The American Journal of Human Genetics.* 84 (6): 740-59

[92] M. Tanaka, et al. (2004) "Mitochondrial Genome Variation in Eastern Asia and the Peopling of Japan," *Genome Research.* 14 (10a): 1832–50

lieved to have developed sometime around 50,000 years ago, somewhere in Asia. The greatest variety of this haplogroup is found in China, indicating that it underwent its earliest diversification in China.[93] The subclade B4b is one of the five haplogroups found in the Native American population.

Haplogroup-R24 is a rare haplogroup found in the Philippines.[94]

Haplogroup-R12 is a rare haplogroup found in Australian Aboriginal peoples.[95] This haplogroup is closely related to the R21 haplogroup of Southeast Asia.

Haplogroup-R21 is found in the Negrito population of Southeast Asia, including the Jahai of Malaysia at 63%,[96] Senoi in Malaysia at 37%, and the Maniq people of Thailand. This haplogroup is closely related to the R12 haplogroup of Australia.

Haplogroup-R14 is found in Papua, Timor, and Lembata in Indonesia.[97]

---

[93] Yong-Gang Yao, et al. (March 2002) "Phylogeographic Differentiation of Mitochondrial DNA in Han Chinese," *American Journal of Human Genetics.* 70(3): 635-651

[94] K. A. Tabbada, et al. (2009) "Philippine Mitochondrial DNA Diversity: A Populated Viaduct between Taiwan and Indonesia?" *Molecular Biology and Evolution.* 27 (1): 21-31

[95] M. J. Pierson, et al. (2006) "Deciphering Past Human Population Movements in Oceania: Provably Optimal Trees of 127 mtDNA Genomes," *Molecular Biology and Evolution.* 23 (10): 1966–75

[96] Catherine Hill, et al. (2006) "Phylogeography and Ethnogenesis of Aboriginal Southeast Asians," *Molecular Biology and Evolution.* 23 (12): 2480-91

[97] S. Mona, et al. (2009) "Genetic Admixture History of Eastern Indonesia as Revealed by Y-Chromosome and Mitochondrial

Haplogroup-R22 is mainly found in Indonesia, with smaller percentages in Thailand, Vietnam, and Cambodia.[98] Within Indonesia, it is found on Bali at 7.3%, and Borneo at 1.9%, as well as on Java, Lombok, Sulawesi, Sumatra, Sumba, and Timor in lower percentages.[99]

Haplogroup-R23 is a rare haplogroup found in Bali and Sumba in Indonesia.[100]

Haplogroup-R30 is mainly found in South Asia, although also found in Japan.[101] Within India, it is found in Andhra Pradesh, the Punjab, and Uttar Pradesh. It is also found in Nepal and Sri Lanka.[102]

Haplogroup-R31 is a rare haplogroup found in Andhra Pradesh,[103] Rajasthan,[104] and Uttar Pradesh,

DNA Analysis," *Molecular Biology and Evolution.* 26 (8): 1865-77
[98] Min-Sheng Peng, et al. (2010) "Tracing the Austronesian Footprint in Mainland Southeast Asia: A Perspective from Mitochondrial DNA," *Molecular Biology and Evolution.* 27 (10): 2417-2430
[99] Catherine Hill, et al. (2007) "A Mitochondrial Stratigraphy for Island Southeast Asia," *The American Journal of Human Genetics.* 80 (1): 29-43
[100] Catherine Hill, et al. (2007) "A Mitochondrial Stratigraphy for Island Southeast Asia," *The American Journal of Human Genetics.* 80 (1): 29-43
[101] Simona Fornarino, et al. (2009) "Mitochondrial and Y-chromosome diversity of the Tharus (Nepal): A reservoir of genetic variation," *BMC Evolutionary Biology.* 9: 154
[102] Gyaneshwer Chaubey, et al. (2008) "Phylogeography of mtDNA haplogroup R7 in the Indian peninsula," *BMC Evolutionary Biology.* 8: 227
[103] Malliya Gounder Palanichamy, et al. (2004) "Phylogeny of Mitochondrial DNA Macrohaplogroup N in India, Based on Complete Sequencing: Implications for the Peopling of South Asia," *The American Journal of Human Genetics.* 75 (6): 966-78.
[104] Gyaneshwer Chaubey, et al. (2008) "Phylogeography of

in India.

Haplogroup-P is widespread throughout Papua,[105] Australia,[106] Melanesia,[107] and Polynesia.[108] Smaller percentages are also found in the Philippines and eastern Indonesia. This group is considered to have formed in Sahul, sometime around 50,000 years ago.[109]

Haplogroup-U is widespread throughout Western Eurasia and North Africa, from South Asia to the Atlantic Ocean. The highest percentages for this haplogroup are found in the Berber and Copts of North Africa, indicating a potential location for the founding group.

Based on the multitude of haplogroups originating from R, it is clear that the founder group for R could have been anywhere in a large swath of Eura-

---

mtDNA haplogroup R7 in the Indian peninsula," *BMC Evolutionary Biology.* 8: 227

[105] J. Friedlaender, et al. (2005) "Expanding Southwest Pacific Mitochondrial Haplogroups P and Q," *Molecular Biology and Evolution.* 22 (6): 1506-17

[106] Georgi Hudjashov, et al. (2007) "Revealing the prehistoric settlement of Australia by Y chromosome and mtDNA analysis," *Proceedings of the National Academy of Sciences.* 104 (21): 8726-30

[107] J. Friedlaender, et al. (2005) "Expanding Southwest Pacific Mitochondrial Haplogroups P and Q," *Molecular Biology and Evolution.* 22 (6): 1506-17

[108] M. Kayser, et al. (2006) "Melanesian and Asian Origins of Polynesians: MtDNA and Y Chromosome Gradients Across the Pacific," *Molecular Biology and Evolution.* 23 (11): 2234-44

[109] Georgi Hudjashov, et al. (2007) "Revealing the prehistoric settlement of Australia by Y chromosome and mtDNA analysis," *Proceedings of the National Academy of Sciences.* 104 (21): 8726-30

sia and North Africa. Europe and Siberia would have to be excluded as Neanderthals were dominant in those regions, and Sahul does not appear to have been colonized until this period, however, it is possible that it was colonized by the Larak civilization. After the fall of Larak, the Laraki people seem to have been migrating in several directions. Those that migrated into Sahul seem to have developed the haplogroup-P mutation by 50,000 years ago. Around the same time, the Larakis that migrated north China seem to have developed the haplogroup-B mutation, that would later become dominant in East Asia, and contribute to the Native American population.

The Larakis that migrated to the west resettled the Middle East after 55,000 years ago[110] began interbreeding with Neanderthals again,[111] and ultimately developed the U and J mutations by 45,000 years ago, which the Sumerian King List suggests was in the Zimbir civilization. Around the same time, another mutation developed in the Laraki that had remained in Southeast Asia, the haplogroup-F mutation. Many additional mutations are listed above, however insufficient research has been published to date to have any clear ideas of when or where these mutations took place.

Meanwhile, the Neanderthals and Denisovans ap-

---

[110] K. A. Hallin, et al. (2012) "Paleoclimate during Neandertal and anatomically modern human occupation at Amud and Qafzeh, Israel: the stable isotope data," *Journal of Human Evolution*, 62(1), 59-73

[111] S. Sankararaman, et al. (2012) "The Date of Interbreeding between Neandertals and Modern Humans," *PLoS Genetics*. 8 (10): e1002947

pear to have begun interbreeding around 90,000 years ago, creating an Altai population of Neanderthals with some Denisovan DNA, that modern-humans would later encounter.[112] A modern-human population began interbreeding with the Altai population around 60,000 years ago,[113] creating one of the ancestral populations for the East Asian and later native American populations.[114] The genetic evidence suggests that Larak was in Southeast Asia, most likely in a region of the Sunda Plateau that is now submerged. Given that the continent of Sahul was colonized during this time, it does seem that there was some level of civilization, as boats would have been required. This does not suggest a particularly advanced civilization but does suggest that they knew how to build houses, and likely had other stone-age technologies, if not something more advanced.

---

[112] Matthew Warren (22 August 2018) "Mum's a Neanderthal, Dad's a Denisovan: First discovery of an ancient-human hybrid - Genetic analysis uncovers a direct descendant of two different groups of early humans," *Nature.* 560 (7719): 417-418

[113] Qiaomei Fu, et al. (2014) "Genome sequence of a 45,000-year-old modern human from western Siberia," *Nature*, Volume 514, Pages 445-449

[114] Q. Ding, et al. (2014) "Neanderthal Introgression at Chromosome 3p21.31 was Under Positive Natural Selection in East Asians," *Molecular Biology and Evolution.* 31 (3): 683-95

Antediluvian Bad-tibira

The Sumerian King List recorded that before Larak, the kingship was in Bad-tibira for the lives of three kings: Enmenluna, Enmengalana, and Dumuzid the Shepherd. As the first two names are translatable as descriptions of eras, it is clear that these were not the names of kings, but rather dynasties or civilizations. These dynasties were listed as spanning the time period of approximately 201,600 to 93,600 years ago. This covers a long span of human pre-history. The first two dynasties of Enmenluna and Enmengalana covered the time-span of 201,600 to 129,600 years ago, which mostly fell within the Penultimate Glacial Period of circa 196,000 to 130,000 years ago.[115] The following dynasty of Dumuzid the Shepherd covered the period of 129,600 to 93,600 years ago, which coincided with the Eemian Interglacial Period of circa 130,000 to 115,000 years ago,[116] and the onset of the Last Glacial Period, which started around 115,000 years ago.

Bad-tibira was also the name of a major Sumerian city in the dynastic period, located at the modern site of Tell al-Madineh, in southern Iraq. Bad-tibira translates as 'fortress of the smiths,'[117] or 'wall of the copper-workers,'[118] which is remarkably similar to

---

[115] Lukas Bicke, et al. (October 2015) "The timing of the penultimate glaciation in the northern Alpine Foreland: new insights from luminescence dating," *Proceedings of the Geologists' Association*, Volume 126, Issues 4-5, Pages 536-550

[116] D. Dahl-Jensen, et al. (2013) "Eemian interglacial reconstructed from a Greenland folded ice core," *Nature*. 493 (7433): 489-94

[117] William W. Hallo and William Kelly Simpson (1974) *The Ancient Near East: A History*, Page 32

[118] W. F. Albright and T. O. Lambdin (1971) "The Evidence of

the root of the name of the Egyptian city of Memphis. The name Memphis is derived from the ancient Egyptian words 'Hut-ka-Ptah,' meaning 'Enclosure of the ka of Ptah.' The term 'ka of Ptah' translates as essentially the 'spirit of Ptah,' or more literally 'craftsmen,' as Ptah was the patron deity of craftsmen. Therefore the name of the city could be read as 'enclosure of the craftsmen,' or 'fortress of the craftsmen.' Like Bad-tibira, Memphis also had a mythical pre-dynastic forebearer with the same name. Archaeological research in dynastic Bad-tibira has been hampered by the fact that the city was destroyed sometime in the Neo-Sumerian era, circa 3575 to 3467 BC ULT (2119 to 2011 BC CMT). The destruction was so devastating that the bricks that remain from before the destruction are vitrified,[119] meaning the fire that destroyed the city was hot enough to melt bricks and wide-spread enough to melt a city. Little else survives from before the city was burnt. After the destruction of the city, King Lippit-Eshtar of Isin rebuilt the Temple of Righteousness in Bad-tibira around 3360 BC ULT (1920 BC CMT),[120] and Governor Sin-Iddinam of Larsa rebuilt the walls of the city around 3270 BC ULT (1830 BC CMT) during the war against the Old Babylonian Empire.

Antediluvian Bad-tibira's kings were listed as Enmenluana, Enmengalana, and Dumuzid the Shep-

---

Language," *The Cambridge Ancient History I*, Part 1, Page 150

[119] Vaughn E. Crawford (1960) "The Location of Bad-Tibira," *Iraq* 22, Page 198

[120] Ferris J. Stephens (1932) "A Newly Discovered Inscription of Libit-Ishtar," *Journal of the American Oriental Society*. 52.2 Page 183

herd. Assyriologists have not agreed on the translation of the names Enmenluana and Enmengalana, mainly as there is justifiably very little interest in arguing the correct translation of a 'mythical' person's name. However, the Sumerians did try to preserve some information, and translating what these names mean is intrinsic to understanding what they left us. The two names are composed of the cuneiform logograms EN, MEN, LU, GAL, and ANA.

EN: can be translated as: dignitary, lord, high priest, ancestor, rule, noble, or time

MEN: is translated as: crown. It is a metaphor implying the EN, meaning ruler.

LU: can be translated as: many, man, men, people, or sheep

GAL: is translated as: great, or big

AN: is translated as: heaven, An (god of heaven), or grain

A: when placed at the end of a word is a nominative.

This means that Enmenluana can be translated as 'the time of the crown of many heavens' although it could also be translated other ways, none of which make any more sense. Enmengalana can be translated as 'the time of the crown of the great heaven.' Neither of which shed much light on the time period, however, this time-span ends with the end of the Penultimate Glacial Period around 130,000 years ago. There are no known surviving stories about either of these kings, however, there is an extensive story about Dumuzid the Shepherd.

Dumuzid the Shepherd

King Dumuzid the Shepherd ruled approximately 129,600 to 93,600 years ago. This means his rule would have begun at the beginning of the Eemian Interglacial Period around 130,000 years ago.[121] During the Eemian Interglacial Period the world warmed as it has in the past 10,000 years, and the glaciers that had been covering the northern continents melted. The Eemian was ultimately warmer than our current world, and the Arctic Ocean became ice-free in the summers, however, Antarctica and Greenland remained glaciated. Wild hippopotamuses, which are currently confined to the African continent, ranged as far north as modern Germany and England.[122] Today the hippopotamus has been hunted to the point that they only survive in remote river regions of Africa, however, a few thousand years ago they ranged throughout almost all of Sub-Saharan Africa, and up to the Mediterranean along the Nile River, and into Canaan.[123]

Dumuzid the Shepherd was a major Sumerian hero and is found in several Sumerian era stories. He was so important that there was a month, in mid-summer, named after him. As the Sumerian calendar is believed to predate the life of the later King Du-

---

[121] D. Dahl-Jensen, et al. (2013) "Eemian interglacial reconstructed from a Greenland folded ice core," *Nature.* 493 (7433): 489-94

[122] Th. van Kolfschoten (2000) "The Eemian mammal fauna of central Europe," *Netherlands Journal of Geosciences.* 79 (2/3): 269-281

[123] Liora Kolska Horwitz and Eitan Tchernov (1990) "Cultural and Environmental Implications of Hippopotamus Bone Remains in Archaeological Contexts in the Levant," *Bulletin of the American Schools of Oriental Research.* 280 (280): 67-76

muzid the Fisher of Uruk, it is clear that they are different people. The original Dumuzid was the inspiration for the later Babylonian and Assyrian god Tammuz, which was also the name of the sixth month on their calendars,[124] which continues to be used in the Hebrew calendar.

In Greece, he was known as Adonis,[125] and the festival for him, in midsummer, was called the Adonia.[126] The name Adonis is believed to originate in Canaan, in the Canaanite word 'adon,' which translates as 'lord.' This belief in Adonis continued to be practiced in Canaan well into the Greek age, as documented by Lucian in his work: On the Syrian Goddess, in the second century AD. Adon continues to be used in the Hebrew language, meaning 'lord,' and when pluralized into 'Adonai' somehow means God. Adonis appears to have been adopted by the Greeks during the Greek dark age through contact with the Canaanites/Phoenicians. There is an older version of him that was apparently inherited from the Mycenaeans, who may have adopted him from the Minoans:[127] Dionysus.

There are also several similarities between the Sumerian myths surrounding Dumuzid and some of the earliest stories in the Tanakh, meaning that the

[124] Jeremy Black and Anthony Green (1992) *Gods, Demons and Symbols of Ancient Mesopotamia: An Illustrated Dictionary.* Page 73-77

[125] Monica S. Cyrino (2010) *Aphrodite, Gods and Heroes of the Ancient World.* Page 95-97

[126] Matthew Dillon (2003) "'Woe for Adonis' – but in Spring, not Summer," *Hermes* 131 (1), Pages 1-9

[127] K. A. Raymoure (2014) "Possible evidence of human sacrifice at Minoan Chania," *Archaeology News Network*

Babylonian era Jews must have had access to these ancient stories. Additional correlations between the stories and festivals of Adonis and the Etruscan Atunis, the Phrygian Attis, and the Egyptian Osiris are well documented.[128] An additional very strong correlation is found between Dumuzid and the ancient Aryan Yima/Yama king/god, even though there is no clear connection between the ancient Sumerians and the ancient Indo-Iranians, meaning that the story of Dumuzid the Shepherd, is very, very old.

---

[128] J. G. Frazer (1906) "Adonis, Attis and Osiris," *Studies in the History of Oriental Religion*, Page 356

The Shepherd and the Smith

Dumuzid the Shepherd is known from various Sumerian epics, four of them form an epic saga: Inanna Prefers the Farmer, Inanna's Descent into the Underworld, The Dream of Dumuzid, and The Return of Dumuzid. Other Dumuzid stories tell alternate versions of the same basic story, with generally minor but sometimes major differences, these stories include Inanna and Bilulu, Dumuzid and Geshtinanna, The Most Bitter Cry, and In the Desert by the Early Grass.

The main epic serial of Dumuzid begins with Inanna Prefers the Farmer, which could be read as either a literal story of a woman choosing one husband over another, or, a metaphorical story explaining why shepherding flocks is better for the earth than engineering canals to water farms. Inanna Prefers the Farmer is also known as Dumuzid and Enkimdu, depending on who is translating it. The story begins with Utu, the Sun, convincing Inanna that she must get married. She courts both Dumuzid the shepherd, and Enkimdu the farmer, and decides to marry Enkimdu, but Utu and Dumuzid gradually persuade her that Dumuzid is the better choice, and ultimately she changes her mind and decides to marry Dumuzid the shepherd.

This story of the Farmer and the Shepherd is the basis of the story in the Judaeo-Christian book of Genesis about Cain and Abel.[129] In Genesis chapter 4, the brothers Cain and Abel each decided to make a

---

[129] Samuel Noah Kramer (1961) *Sumerian Mythology: A Study of Spiritual and Literary Achievement in the Third Millennium B.C.*: Revised Edition

sacrifice to the god Yahweh, Cain from the crops he'd grown, and Abel from one of the sheep he was shepherding. Yahweh for some reason refused Cain's vegetables which caused Cain to become so angry that he killed Abel, which then confused Yahweh because he couldn't find Abel. However, Cain felt guilty, and so to make sure no one killed Cain, Yahweh 'marked' him. It is unclear what this is a reference to, however, several ancient authors claimed it was a disease that caused 'groaning and tremors,' which was the translation used in the original version of the Christian Old Testament.[130] This may have been a reference to the diseases that many metal-smiths had in ancient times, which was caused by arsenic poisoning. Many ancient gods associated with metal-smithing were described as having limps or other health problems.[131]

Cain ran away from Eden, where Yahweh was living, to the land of Nod, and built a city called Enoch, the first city in the Judaeo-Christian timeline. While it is possible the later Jewish story only drew the most basic premise for the Cain and Abel story from Dumuzid and Enkimdu, it is also possible that the Babylonian Jews drew on sources we no longer have.

---

[130] John Byron (2011) *Cain and Abel in text and tradition: Jewish and Christian interpretations of the first sibling rivalry.* Page 98

[131] K. Aterman (5 March, 1999) "From Horus the child to Hephaestus who limps: a romp through history," *American Journal Medical Genetics.* 83(1):53-63

The Mountain in the Steppes

In order to understand these stories, it is impera-
tive to understand the language being used, and
what the various names mean. Dumuzid is derived
from the Sumerian words DU MU meaning 'son of,'
and ZI meaning 'life,' making Dumuzid's name mean
'Son of Life.' In the early dynastic period, Dumuzid
was also called Ishtaran in the cities of Nippur and
Der. Ishtaran's consort was called Sharrat-Deri
meaning 'the Queen of Der.' The name Ishtaran may
be a remnant of the older Kish civilization's name
for Dumuzid, as it sounds like Ishtar, which the
Sumerians called Inanna. Ishtar is generally considered to be a Semitic name, as there are a variety of
Semitic variations including the Aramaic Attar,
South Arabian Athtar, Amharic Astar, Moabite
Ashtar, and Ugaritic At'tar. Some of these variations
of Attar were male, while others were female, which
is consistent with other Semitic gods which changed
gender depending on whether the local clan was pa-
triarchal or matriarchal.

Inanna's name is believed to mean 'Lady of
Heaven,'[132] however, the Sumerian cuneiform logograms do not translate as that,[133] and she is therefore interpreted by Assyriologists as a goddess that
was adopted into the Sumerian religion from another culture. According to the Sumerian epic sagas
Lugal Banda and the Mountain Cave and Lugal
Banda and the Anzu Bird, the goddess Inanna moved
to Uruk during the life of Lugal Banda of Uruk,

---

[132] T. Abusch (2000) "Ištar." *Nin* 1: 23-7
[133] Gwendolyn Leick (1998) *A Dictionary of Ancient Near Eastern Mythology*, Page 86-87

sometime around 9124 BC ULT. Prior to relocating to Uruk, Inanna was in the land of Aratta, somewhere northeast of Uruk, past the Zagros Mountains. Aratta was also mentioned in the Baudhayana Sutra, an ancient Sanskrit text, most likely compiled between 800 and 600 BC,[134] although Aratta's location was not given. In both cases, lapis lazuli was mentioned in connection with Aratta, which suggests Aratta was in the Badakhshan region of modern Afghanistan and Tajikistan, as most of the lapis lazuli mined in the ancient world was mined in Badakhshan.[135] While this story of Lugal Banda is generally considered a myth, as no definitive proof has been found of Aratta's existence, it would explain why Inanna has a non-Sumerian name.

Dumuzid's sister was recorded as being Geshtinanna, and his mother's name was recorded as Sirtur, although the name of his father has not survived. Geshtinanna's name translates as approximately 'wine/vine of the heavens.'[136] In the later Akkadian and the Assyrian and Babylonian religions, she became the goddess Belet-Seri, which translates as 'Lady of the Steppes.' Belet-Seri was also called the 'scribe of the Earth,' and after marrying the god Amurru became known as the 'queen of the deserts.' The cuneiform logogram for the Akkadian word 'seri,' was the Sumerian logogram EDIN, which was the Sumerian word for 'steppe.' The Sumerian Garden-of-the-Gods is theorized to be the

---

[134] Kim Plofker (2007) *Mathematics in India.* Page 17

[135] Peter Roger Moorey (1999) *Ancient mesopotamian materials and industries: the archaeological evidence.* Pages 86-87

[136] D. O. Edzard (1957-71) "Geštinanna," *Reallexikon der Assyriologie und Vorderasiatischen Archäologie.* 3, Pages 299-301

basis of the later Jewish Garden of Eden,[137] where the name Eden was based on the Sumerian logogram EDIN. In several Sumerian stories such as Debate Between Sheep and Grain, Enki and Ninhursag, and Song of the Hoe the Garden-of-the-Gods is described as being on a mountain, surrounded by a steppe explaining how the word 'edin' would have been associated with the story.

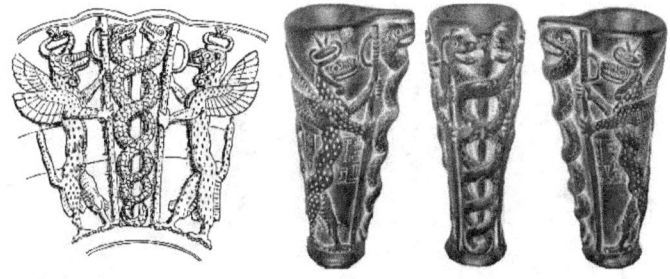

Geshtinanna's Akkadian name Belet-Seri, records she began as King Dumuzid's sister, as the 'Lady of Edin,' then she married Amurru, and became the Queen of the Desert. Amurru, called Martu in Sumerian, was a Semitic god and was the primary god of the Amorites. Like Dumuzid, he was also called 'the shepherd,' which implies he was also a leader. He was also called 'belu shadi' meaning 'lord of the mountain,' which is the origin of the later Jewish phrase 'El Shaddai,' meaning 'god of the mountain.'[138] Amurru was also called several variations of

---

[137] Samuel Noah Kramer (1964) *The Sumerians: Their History, Culture and Character.* Page 293

[138] L. R. Bailey (1968) "Israelite 'Ēl šadday and Amorite Bêl šadê," *Journal of Biblical Literature.* 87, 434-38

'belu shadi,' including 'dur-hur-sag-ga sikil-a-ke' meaning 'he who dwells on the pure mountain' and 'kur-za-gan ti-[la],' which means 'who inhabits the shining mountain.' The implication is that Geshti-nanna married Martu, while they lived on the mountain in the steppes, and Martu ruled after Dumuzid died, but the steppes became a desert.

Geshtinanna was also said to be married to Nin-Gishzida,[139] a strange character similar to Ishtaran's companion Nirah. Nin-Gishzada is a title that translates as 'Lady of the Good Tree,' in Sumerian, however, was depicted as male. Many Sumerian female deities appear to have been emasculated as the Akkadians subsumed the Sumerian civilization. Nin-Gishzada and Nirah were both depicted in Sumerian art as a snake, or as an anthropomorphize snake. The modern caduceus symbols, used to represent both

[139] F. Wiggermann (1998-2001) "Nin-ĝišzida," *Reallexikon der Assyriologie und vorderasiatischen Archäologie.* 9, Pages 368-373

medicine and commerce are derived, via the Greeks, from an ancient Sumerian emblem in which the two serpents are entwined around the Good Tree, accompanied by the two Guardian dragons, pictured above on the Libation vase of Gudea.

The Guardian dragons, which the Sumerians called Mushhus, and were later called Mushhushshu by the Akkadians, Babylonians, and Assyrians, were the Guardians of the Good Tree. On the opposite page are a couple of photographs showing the Gate of Ishtar as it was in the 1920s, and a Mushhushshu on a modern reconstruction of the Gate of Ishtar. The Gate of Ishtar was one of the gates to Babylon built in 575 BC. This is a clear forerunner of the Tree of Knowledge in the Jewish Garden of Eden. Like in the Sumerian story, the Jewish story has a snake associated with the sacred tree, which, like Nin-Gishzada, could speak. The Guardians also showed up in the Jewish story, as the two cherubs at the entrance to Eden, who were posted there to keep out humanity after Eve was convinced by the serpent to eat the sacred fruit, and then gave some to Adam.[140] In the Book of Ezekiel the cherubs are described as being winged creatures combining human, lion, bull, and eagle features,[141] much like the Assyrian and Babylonian era depictions of Mushhushshu.

The second serpent in the original caduceus was Amashilama, Nin-Gishzada's sister. Similar iconography of a pair of snake-people at the dawn of history is depicted in several ancient cultures, including Fuxi and Nuwa from China, and Osiris and Isis from

---

[140] *Genesis* Chapter 3
[141] *Ezekiel* Chapters 9-10

Egypt. Below are a rubbing of a pictorial brick from the Eastern Han Dynasty, in China circa 25 to 220 AD, and a photograph close-up of Fuxi and Nuwa. The pictorial brick also includes several other features of ancient Chinese religion, including the Peach Tree of Immortality, and the Great Bear, who is similar to Jambavan from the Indian epics.

Isis doesn't appear to have been depicted as a serpent until the New Kingdom, when she merged with the Egyptian Old Kingdom god Renenutet, becoming known as Isis-Renenutet. On the opposite is an excerpt from the New Kingdom book *Amduat* (left) which depicts both Isis and Nephtys as serpents, along with a Greco-Roman era Egyptian carving (right) of Isis-Renenutet, Serapis, and the baby Horus. Renenutet was a similar, yet reptilian, mother-goddess that dates back to pre-Dynastic times in Egypt.

Osiris was replaced by Serapis as Isis consort during the Greek era, who was a merged god, combining Osiris and the Old Babylonian god Ea, previously known as Enki by the Sumerians. Ea was known as Shar Apsi in Neo-Babylonian, meaning 'King of the Apsu.' The reason the Greeks believed Osiris and Enki were originally the same god is unclear, however, they did have ancient Egyptian and Babylonian texts that we no longer have access to.

These snake twins also seem to be the root of the story found in the Mahabharata of the two giant poisonous serpents in Indra's heaven that were stationed as Guardians of the amrita, the elixir of immortality. This is reminiscent of the Jewish version of the story, where the cherubs were placed at the entrance to Eden to stop humanity from eating from a second sacred tree: the Tree of Life, which would make humans immortal if they ate from it. While snake-people and dragons guarding a tree growing immortality-fruit makes the story of Dumuzid seem like fiction, it is nevertheless, even if it is fiction, certainly an ancient story embedded in many ancient cultures, and continues to influence the modern Abrahamic religions.

Above are two photos showing statues of Renenutet (left) and a similar Ubaid era reptilian mother-goddess (right) from Mesopotamia, dating to between 8331 and 5831 BC ULT (6500 to 4000 BC CMT).

Jewish Antediluvian Bloodlines

In the Jewish story of Cain and Abel, the two brothers fought for the approval of Yahweh, and Cain ultimately killed Abel. Cain is written in Hebrew as קֵין and is translated in the King James Bible as either Cain or Kenite depending on the translator's choice. The Kenites were a tribe that lived in southern Canaan during the time of Abraham and Moses, whose name translates as Smiths, and are reported to have been copper-smiths.[142] They are believed to be the descendants of Cain in some interpretations of Jewish timelines.[143] While Cain is generally assumed to be the son of Adam, many ancient Jewish scholars[144] such as Philo[145] and Pirke DeRabbi Eliezer[146] believed he was the son of the serpent from the garden of Eden, called Samael, whose name means 'Venom of God.'

In the book of Genesis, Cain named the city Enoch after his son, who apparently isn't the Enoch that later encountered the Watchers, but a different Enoch. The book of Genesis describes two genealo-

---

[142] Stephen L. Harris (1985) *Understanding the Bible*

[143] Archibald Henry Sayce (1899) "Kenites," *A Dictionary of the Bible*. II. Page 834

[144] Louis Ginzberg (1909) *The Legends of the Jews Vol I: The Ten Generations - The Birth of Cain*

[145] John Byron (2011) *Cain and Abel in text and tradition: Jewish and Christian interpretations of the first sibling rivalry*. Page 98

[146] Gerard P. Luttikhuizen, editor (2003) *Eve's Children: The Biblical Stories Retold and Interpreted in Jewish and Christian traditions*, Volume 5, Page vii

gies descending from Adam and Eve, the genealogy of Seth, and the genealogy of Cain. These two blood-lines both have people named Enoch and Lamech, and most of the names are similar in both genealo-gies. Theologians have suggested that the two blood-lines represent two competing pre-Judaic bloodlines, the Sethite and Cainite bloodlines. It is believed by many that the Sethite bloodline is inspired by the Sumerian Antediluvian Dynasties.[147]

Cainite bloodline:

- Adam
- Cain
- Enoch
- Irad
- Mehujael
- Methusael
- Lamech
- Naamah

Sethite bloodline:

- Adam
- Seth
- Enosh
- Cainan
- Mahalaleel

---

[147] Dianne Bergant and Robert J. Karris (1992) "Genesis," *The Collegeville Bible Commentary: Old Testament*. Pages 46-47

- Jared

- Enoch

- Methuselah

- Lamech

- Noah

Sumerian Antediluvian dynasties:

- Alulim

- Alalgar

- Enmenluna

- Enmengalanna

- Dumuzid

- Ensipaziana

- Enmendurana

- Ubara-Tutu

If the Sethite bloodline was inspired by the Sumerian King List, then it is logical to assume that the very similar Cainite bloodline must have been inspired by the Sumerian King List as well. In fact given the similarities in the names, the two must have had a common ancestral bloodline. This has been reconstructed as the combined bloodline:

- Adam

- Seth-Cain/Cainan

- Enosh-Mehujael/Mahalaleel

- Irad/Jared

- Enoch

- Methusael/Methuselah

- Lamech

- Naamah/Noah

In this combined bloodline, Seth and Cain are still the sons of Adam, and Cainan is an alternate name for Cain. Enosh would be the cousin of Mehujael, who is also Mahalaleel. Irad and Jared are the same person, and father on Enoch, whose son is Methusael or Methuselah, who is the father of Lamech, who is the father of Naamah or Noah. Naturally, this cannot be proven as thousands of years have passed since the two bloodlines were recombined into *Genesis*, however, it does show that the story of these patriarchs was very old by the time the early Jews were compiling *Genesis*.

The story of Cain and Abel does include some other details which could descend from an older account of *Dumuzid and Enkimdu*. In the Jewish story, Abel was the shepherd who died, like Dumuzid the Shepherd. After that Cain went east to the land of Nod and built the city of Enoch. While Cain's name indicates he was a smith, as one would expect if he came from Bad-tibira, the book of Genesis claims the city he founded was the City of Enoch. If one accepts the correlation between King Enmendurana and the idea both Enochs were divergent stories of the same Enoch, then the city Cain founded was Zimbir, which would later rise to prominence between 65,000 and 43,000 years ago.

This city of Enoch was built in the land of Nod,

'on the east of Eden' according to Genesis 4:16. Based on the correlation of Eden and 'edin,' the Sumerian word for steppe, the land of Nod would have been somewhere on the same steppe as the mountain where the Garden-of-the-Gods was. Nod translates as approximately Wanderers, implying that whoever was living there were nomadic, explaining why Cain had to build his own city. Naturally, there are the internal contradictions within the Genesis narrative, in which there are three people in the world, Adam, Eve, and Cain, and Cain goes off on his own and has a child, then builds a city for that child. Clearly whoever wrote this, and whoever edited it, and whoever compiled it into what is today the book of Genesis, knew there had to be other people around.

Recent Out of Africa Theory?

If one accepts the Recent Out-of-Africa theory for modern-human origin in Africa, then the lifespan of Dumuzid was during the first phase of modern-human migrations out of Africa into the Middle East and South Asia. The current version of the Recent Out of Africa theory proposes that modern-humans first migrated into southern Eurasia between 110,000 and 95,000 years ago,[148] and by 100,000 years ago modern-humans and Neanderthals had begun inter-breeding.[149] Meanwhile Dumuzid's lifespan was listed as approximately 129,600 to 93,600 years ago. Given that Cain was leaving Eden traveling east, the original Garden-of-the-Gods must have been in North Africa somewhere. As Zimbir was required to still exist in 65,000 and 44,000 years ago, the City of Enoch would have to have been in South Asia. This would then suggest that Cain settling in Nod, and being 'marked' as different from other people, was the first wave of modern-humans settling in southern Eurasia and creating light-skinned children with the native Neanderthals. The light-skin genes in modern Eurasian and Native American populations are believed to be inherited from Neanderthal ancestors.[150]

---

[148] Rachel Lentz (September 22, 2016) "Past climate swings orchestrated early human migration waves out of Africa," phys.org

[149] Martin Kuhlwilm, et al. (25 February 2016) "Ancient gene flow from early modern humans into Eastern Neanderthals," *Nature*. 530, Pages 429-33

[150] C. Lalueza-Fox (2007) "A Melanocortin 1 Receptor Allele Suggests Varying Pigmentation Among Neanderthals," *Science*.

This is of course, only valid if the current version of the Recent Out-of-Africa theory is correct. Modern-human remains have been found in Eurasia long predating the current version of the Recent Out of Africa theory, indicating that modern-humans either ventured out of Africa earlier than previously thought, or that they originated elsewhere. The immediate ancestor of the modern humans was thought to be homo-heidelbergensis until genetic analysis of the Sima de los Huesos fossils showed homo-heidelbergensis to be primitive Neanderthals, and pushed back the splitting of the modern-human and heidelbergensis-neanderthal bloodlines to roughly 600,000 to 800,000 years ago.[151] This raises the question of who our primary ancestors were if they weren't homo-heidelbergensis. The ancestor species of homo-heidelbergensis is currently believed to be homo-erectus, which could be the last common ancestor the modern-human bloodline had with the Neanderthal and Denisovan bloodlines.

Homo-erectus ranged over most of the African and Eurasian landmass, however, they were replaced across that entire range by homo-heidelbergensis by 500,000 years ago. One of the last homo-erectus enclaves is believed to be in Java, Indonesia from around 143,000 years ago.[152] Another later enclave was found in Bilzingsleben, Germany from around

---

318 (5855): 1453-55

[151] Matthias Meyer, et al. (24 March 2016) "Nuclear DNA sequences from the Middle Pleistocene Sima de los Huesos hominins," *Nature*. 531, pages 504-507

[152] E. Indriati, et al. (2011) "The Age of the 20 Meter Solo River Terrace, Java, Indonesia and the Survival of Homo erectus in Asia," *PLoS ONE* 6(6): e21562.

370,000 years ago.[153] Somewhere, modern-humans are assumed to have evolved from homo-erectus or an intermediate species, and by 200,000 years ago seem to have spanned a vast region of Africa and Eurasia.

Modern-human teeth discovered in the Qesem Cave, in Israel, have been dated to between 400,000 and 200,000 years old, and appear to be physiologically similar to the remains found in the Qafzah and Es Skhul Caves, in Israel, dated to between 120,000 and 80,000 years ago.[154] In Morocco, the remains recovered from the Jereb Irhoud Cave have been dated to between 350,000 and 280,000 years ago.[155] In Dali County, Shaanxi, China, the so-called Dali-Man remains have been recovered, which have not been dated themselves, however, ox teeth recovered with the Dali-Man remains have been dated via uranium-series dating to 260,000 years ago.[156] The fact that the Dali-Man remains were recovered with ox remains indicates that humans could have had domesticated cattle a quarter million years earlier than generally assumed. Dali-Man has been described as being either early homo-sapiens or late homo-erectus, indicating a potential transitional species in Eastern

---

[153] D Mania and U Mania (1988) "Deliberate engravings on bone artefacts of Homo Erectus," *Rock Art Research.* 5, 91-97

[154] I. Hershkovitz, et al. (April 2011) "Middle pleistocene dental remains from Qesem Cave (Israel)," *American Journal of Physical Anthropology,* 144 (4)

[155] Ewan Callaway (7 June 2017) "Oldest Homo sapiens fossil claim rewrites our species' history," *Nature.*

[156] J. L. Xiao, et al. (2002) "Age of the Fossil Dali Man in North-Central China deduced from Chronostratigraphy of the Loess-paleosol Sequence," *Quaternary Science Reviews.* 21 (20): 2191-2198

Asia.

Between 200,000 and 100,000 years ago a large number of modern-human sites appear across Eurasia and Africa, calling into question why anyone would support the recent Out of Africa theory. By 177,000 years ago modern-humans were living in Israel,[157] the UAE by 127,000 years ago,[158] China by 120,000 years ago,[159] and Oman by 106,000 years ago.[160] The reason that the recent Out of Africa theory has support is due to the limited genetic diversity found among non-Africans compared to the genetic diversity found on the African continent. Genetic studies from the early 2000s showed higher levels of genetic diversity within Africa than in the rest of the world,[161] however larger studies conducted since then have shown that the Eurasian and Oceanic populations were driven by natural selection to selectively breed out certain traits,[162] and the greater diversity within Africa was caused by

---

[157] Ankita Mehta (26 January 2018) "A 177,000-year-old jawbone fossil discovered in Israel is oldest human remains found outside Africa," *International Business Times*

[158] Simon J. Armitage (January 2011) "The southern route "out of Africa": evidence for an early expansion of modern humans into Arabia," *Science*. 331 (6016): 453-6

[159] Christopher J. Bae, et al. (8 December 2017) "On the origin of modern humans: Asian perspectives," *Science*. 358 (6368)

[160] J. I. Rose, et al. (2011) "The Nubian Complex of Dhofar, Oman: an African middle stone age industry in Southern Arabia," *PLoS ONE*. 6 (11): e28239

[161] Ning Yu, et al. (May 2002) "Larger Genetic Differences Within Africans Than Between Africans and Eurasians," *Genetics*. 161 (1): 269-274.

[162] G. Coop, et al. (June 2009) "The role of geography in human adaptation," *PLoS Genetics*. 5 (6): e1000500.

Eurasians migrating into Africa.[163]

At least one human species was apparently living in North America by 130,000 years ago.[164] Given that other animals were able to cross between Siberia and Alaska, it seems illogical that archaic humans couldn't have. The dominant genes in the Native American population are modern-human, like the rest of the planet's population, however, there are traces of both Neanderthal and Denisovan DNA found in the Americas. The Neanderthal DNA is easy to explain, as all native Americans have some Neanderthal DNA inherited from their Eurasian ancestors.

The Denisovan DNA is more difficult to explain, as it is found in the northern Andes, in South America. If the Denisovan alleles were carried into the Americas by migrants from Eurasia traveling with the other migrants, the Denisovan DNA would be spread through the entire native American population, and not contained in a region of South America. Either a group of modern-humans with a higher percentage of Denisovan DNA migrated into the Americas before the rest of the ancestors of the Native Americans, or the Denisovans migrated into the Americas, and didn't settle or survive in North America. As the Denisovan DNA in the Asia-Pacific region is focused on the equator, it is possible that

---

[163] Deepti Gurdasani, et al. (July 2015) "The African Genome Variation Project shapes medical genetics in Africa," *Nature.* 517 (7534): 327-332

[164] Ewen Callaway (26 April, 2017) "Controversial study claims humans reached Americas 100,000 years earlier than thought," *Nature*

the Denisovans didn't like the cold, meaning the extreme cold of the glacial periods, that covered most of North America in ice-sheets miles high, could have driven the Denisovans south. The time period of the ancient human presence in North America does happen to correlate with the beginning of the Eemian Interglacial Period around 130,000 years ago, and coincidentally perhaps, the beginning of Dumuzid's reign on the Sumerian King List.

The Underworld in the Mountain

Regardless of where modern-humans originated, they were widespread by 200,000 years ago, and while the Sumerian Edin could be interpreted as North Africa, various Eurasian stories point to the Eurasian steppes. Wherever Dumuzid's Bad-tibira was, his story wasn't about his city, but rather, his death. His story continues in the epic poem Inanna's Descent into the Underworld, in which Inanna visited her sister Eresh-Kigal in the Underworld, to attend the funeral of Eresh-Kigal's husband Gugalanna. Eresh-Kigal's name translates as 'Queen of the Great Earth,' and she lived in a place called Ganzir in the Kur, with her husband Gugalanna, before his death.

Kur was the Sumerian word meaning 'mountain,' although in the later Sumerian period her abode became known as Irkalla. The Akkadians later called it Ersetu, their word for the ground, or used the various Sumerian euphemisms as names.[165] Irkalla meant 'bringer of precious wealth,' which seems to be the same meaning as the Greco-Roman Plouton/Pluto whose name meant 'wealth,' and referred to the mineral wealth that miners pulled from the Earth.[166] The Sumerians also used several euphemisms for Kur in later Sumerian stories, which translate as 'House of Dumuzi,' 'Mountain of No Return,' 'Dark-

---

[165] Jeremy Black and Anthony Green (1992) *Gods, Demons and Symbols of Ancient Mesopotamia: An Illustrated Dictionary*, Page 180-187

[166] William Hansen (2005) *Classical Mythology: A Guide to the Mythical World of the Greeks and Romans*, Page 182

ness', or simply 'Great Earth.' Below is an Assyrian stela depicting Ishtar (Inanna) riding a lion. Below is a photograph of the Queen of Night Relief dating to the Old Babylonian Empire, circa 3352 to 3038 BC ULT (1894 to 1595 BC CMT), believed to either depict Eresh-Kigal or Ishtar (Inanna) standing on lions.

During the Sumerian era, Ganzir was described as a dark, dreary cavern located deep below the ground,[167] where inhabitants were believed to continue 'a shadowy version of life on earth.'[168] This underworld was no fiery abode, like the Greek Underworld. It was dark, boring, and the food was described as dry as dust with bread as hard as clay. It also didn't matter what someone had done before going to the Underworld, the conditions were the same for everyone.

Eresh-Kigal's husband was Gugalanna during the Sumerian era, but was replaced by Nergal during the later Akkadian, Babylonian, and Assyrian eras. Gugalanna's name is also a title, which translates as 'canal-inspector of heaven,' an odd title for someone in the Underworld. The name Ganzir is also odd, it is made up of the logograms GAN and ZIR, which translates as approximately 'foundation water-pump,' which when combined with Gugalanna's title makes this Underworld sound more like a subterranean water pumping station. Nergal was described during the Akkadian and Old Babylonian eras as the god of drought, indicating he may be the same character as the failed 'canal-inspector' Gugalanna. From there he evolved through the Neo-Babylonian era into a god of plague and pestilence, and took over the rule of the Underworld from his wife.[169]

---

[167] C. E. Barret (2007) "Was dust their food and clay their bread?: Grave goods, the Mesopotamian afterlife, and the liminal role of Inana/Ištar," *Journal of Ancient Near Eastern Religions*, 7 (1): 7-65

[168] M. Choksi (2014) "Ancient Mesopotamian Beliefs in the Afterlife," *Ancient History Encyclopedia*

[169] Maciej M. Munnich (2013) *The God Resheph in the Ancient*

The Dumuzid Saga

In the epic Inanna's Descent into the Underworld, Inanna decides to visit Ganzir, which seems like an odd thing to do, if the Underworld referred to the state of being dead. As the law stated that no one could leave Ganzir other than messengers from Ganzir, she ordered her minister Nin-Shubur to intercede with the gods Anu, Enki, Enlil, and Nanna if she wasn't back within three days.[170] Nin-Shubur translates as 'Lady of the East,' and as minister of Inanna she could apparently speak directly with the gods, implying this civilization was a pantheocracy, like the later Sumerian civilization. Early Assyriologists assumed she was male, because women weren't allowed in government when 'modern' Assyriologists first discovered references to her, and the Akkadian version of her was a male: Papsukkal the messenger of the gods.[171] However this concept was proven in error, and she is now considered female again.[172]

Inanna dressed up in her most elaborate attire in order to impress everyone in Ganzir, and headed down to the gates of Ganzir, but when she got there she was stripped of her fancy clothes and her lapis lazuli measuring rod, which appears to be an archaic

Near East. Pages 62-63

[170] Charles Penglase (1994) *Greek Myths and Mesopotamia: Parallels and Influence in the Homeric Hymns and Hesiod.* Page 157-9

[171] Jeremy Black and Anthony Green (1992) *Gods, Demons and Symbols of Ancient Mesopotamia: An Illustrated Dictionary,* Page 141

[172] Diane Wolkstein (1983) "Sumerian Goddess," *The New York Review of Books*

precursor to the royal scepter.[173] Apparently her fancy clothes and measuring rod weren't permitted in Ganzir, where everyone was dressed in filthy rags, and so she had to proceed into Ganzir naked. When she reached her sister's palace she was apparently quite angry about it and tried to oust Eresh-Kigal, ordering her to relinquish her throne. Unfortunately for her the seven judges of Ganzir, turned against her and ended up hanging her naked body from a hook, leaving Eresh-Kigal on the throne.[174]

After three days minister Nin-Shubur went to the temples of An, Enki, Enlil, and Nanna, begging them to free Inanna from the Underworld. An, Enlil, and Nanna all refuse to intercede as Inanna knew the law before heading down to Ganzir, but the compassionate Enki decided to help. Enki sent two androgynous beings down into Ganzir to heal Eresh-Kigal, and ask her for Inanna's body. These two androgynous beings were named Galatura and Kurjara, and while they are described as androids made from the dirt under Enki's fingernails in the oldest surviving version of Inanna Descends to the Underworld, the name Galatura betrays a plausible earlier version of the story. The logograms GA-LA, and TU-RA translate as 'Priest of the Sick.'

During the Sumerian era, the priests at the Temple of Inanna at Uruk were called galas. This priesthood was composed of both cis-gender women and

---

[173] Diane Wolkstein and Samuel Noah Kramer (1983) *Inanna: Queen of Heaven and Earth: Her Stories and Hymns from Sumer,* Page 56

[174] Jeremy Black, et al. (2003-2006) "Inana's descent to the netherworld," *Electronic Text Corpus of Sumerian Literature*

transgender women, or in older translations transvestites.[175] Transgender priests were common in ancient Sumerian temples[176] and continued to be common in the Middle East until the Roman period. During the Roman Republican era, the Cult of Cybele was adopted into the Roman pantheon, in 204 BC.[177]

[175] Jean Bottéro and H. Petschow (1972-1975) "Homosexualität," *Reallexikon der Assyriologie und Vorderasiatischen Archäologie*, 4:459b-468b

[176] Gwendolyn Leick (1994) *Sex and Eroticism in Mesopotamian Literature*

[177] Luther H. Martin (1987) *Hellenistic Religions: An Introduction.* Page 83

Above is a photograph of a Sumerian statue of gala priests. The priests of Cybele were called gallus, and they were described as eunuchs that dressed as women,[178] which in modern terminology would be trans-gender women. These gallus worshiped Cybele and her mate Attis, which was the Phrygian version of Adonis,[179] himself a later version of Dumuzid the Shepherd. This means that the belief in Dumuzid and Inanna was not just widespread, but lasted a long time.

When Enki sent the two priests to Eresh-Kigal, she was described as being very sick, in agony like a woman giving birth. They were advised to offer to help her if she agreed to give them Inanna's body. Enki provided Kurjara with the food-of-live, and Galatura with the water-of-life. Then he instructed them to sprinkle the food-of-life and water-of-life over Inanna's body to bring her back to life.

This odd instruction from Enki served as the basis of the later Akkadian, Babylonian, and Assyrian Tammuz festivals, as well as the identical Adonia in Greece. In these midsummer festivals women would sprinkle seeds and water them, which would cause them to sprout, but then die as it was too late in the season for them to grow. Similar festivals were practiced by the Etruscan for Atunis and the Egyptians for Osiris. Why so many ancient cultures wasted seeds like this in midsummer is unknown, but it was practiced over a large territory for thousands of years. It is also reminiscent of the Christian Eu-

---

[178] Maarten J. Vermaseren (1977) *Cybele and Attis: the myth and the cult*, translated by A. M. H. Lemmers, Page 115

[179] James Frazer (1906–15) *The Golden Bough*, Chapter 34

charist, in which eating a cracker, representing human flesh, and drinking some wine, representing human blood, grants immortality... after you die.

While this story is central to the ancient returning from death rituals of many religions, it could also be interpreted slightly differently. While the oldest surviving version does portray Inanna as dying after the judges yelled at her, hanging a dead body on a hook does seem like beating a dead horse. Why torture a corpse? If she wasn't actually dead, giving her food and water after removing her from the hook does seem like the logical thing to do.

When the judges saw her heading back up to the surface, they stated that as no one was allowed to leave Ganzir, she would have to have someone take her place. They sent a number of 'galla' with her to make sure she sent someone back to Ganzir to take her place. The word 'galla' is often translated as 'demon' by Assyriologists, especially in relation to Ganzir, and that does seem to be how the Akkadians and later Mesopotamian civilizations interpreted the term. Nevertheless, the term is composed of the Sumerian logograms GAL and LA, meaning 'great man,' and was the Sumerian term for their concept of a policeman, deputy, or bailiff.[180] Translating the term as bailiff does make more sense, as these 'galla' were sent by a group of judges, to make sure someone that was essentially on probation carried through on her agreement to send someone down into the Ganzir to take her place. Nevertheless, this term did evolve into the Akkadian 'galla,' meaning

---

[180] John A. Halloran (December 10, 2006) *Sumerian Lexicon* Version 3.0, gal5-lá

demon in the contemporary Judaeo-Christian-Islamic and Buddhist concept of the term.

Outside the gates of Ganzir, Inanna and the bailiffs found the minister Nin-Shubur waiting for her to return. The bailiffs wanted to take Nin-Shubur back to Ganzir as her substitute, but Inanna refused to let them, stating Nin-Shubur was too loyal. Next, they found Shara, Inanna's brother, who the bailiffs wanted to take. Inanna objected stating he was her 'singer, manicurist, and hairdresser,' who was still mourning, and so Inanna wouldn't let the bailiffs take Shara. Then they found Inanna's other brother Lulal, who was still mourning, so Inanna wouldn't let them take him either.

Then they found Dumuzid sitting on the throne, apparently not grieving the loss of Inanna, and in a fit of rage, she told the bailiffs to take Dumuzid to Ganzir. In some of the later versions they found Dumuzid being entertained by a slave-girl, however, this seems to be a late addition to the story.

The story continued in the Sumerian poem *The Dream of Dumuzid*, in which Dumuzid told his sister Geshtinanna a dream he'd had.[181] In the dream Dumuzid escaped the bailiffs who were trying to take him to Ganzir, and they began searching Bad-tibira for him. They interrogated his sister Geshtinanna, but she would not tell them where he was hiding. Then they interrogated one of his friends who gave up Dumuzid's hiding place. The bailiffs captured him

---

[181] Diane Wolkstein and Samuel Noah Kramer (1983) *Inanna: Queen of Heaven and Earth: Her Stories and Hymns from Sumer*, Page 74-78

and dragged him to Ganzir.[182] This poem may also be a later addition to the saga, however, is generally included as it fits between *Inanna's Descent into the Underworld* and *The Return of Dumuzid.*

The Return of Dumuzid picks up where *The Dream of Dumuzid* ends: Dumuzid had been taken to Ganzir, and Geshtinanna was bereaved. Geshtinanna and Dumuzid's mother Sirtur were lamenting the loss of Dumuzid, when Inanna joined them, regretting her rashness in letting the bailiffs take Dumuzid. They decided to visit Dumuzid in Ganzir, and while there Inanna arranged for Geshtinanna and Dumuzid to each spend only half the year in Ganzir, and be free the rest of the year.[183]

---

[182] Steve Tinney (April 2018) "Dumuzi's Dream" Revisited," *Journal of Near Eastern Studies,* 77 (1): 85-89

[183] Charles Penglase (1994) *Greek Myths and Mesopotamia: Parallels and Influence in the Homeric Hymns and Hesiod.* Page 84

Ishtar and Tammuz, and Zababa

The Akkadian and Babylonian version of Inanna and Dumuzid was Ishtar and Tammuz. This version drew the most directly and demonstrably from the Sumerian version, as the Akkadians literally lived in Sumerian cities, and they adopted Sumerian gods and heroes into their pantheon, either adding them as new gods or syncretizing them with existing Semitic gods. As the Babylonians and Assyrians were the cultural descendants of the Akkadians they inherited these gods, yet expanded and changed the pantheons over time.

The largest difference between the Sumerian and Akkadian-Babylonian narratives of Ishtar versus Inanna revolves around Eresh-Kigal's husband. In the Sumerian era Eresh-Kigal's husband was Gugalanna,[184] who was sometimes represented as being alive, and subservient to his wife, but by the time of *Inanna Descends to the Underworld* was dead, and was the reason Inanna was entering Ganzir, to attend his funeral. In the Akkadian and Babylonian era, Eresh-Kigal's husband Nergal was alive and they rule the Underworld together.[185] The Babylonian story *Nergal and Eresh-Kigal* tells the story of how these gods met and ended up married. This story dates back to at least 1350 BC, as a copy of it was recovered from Tel El-Amarna in Egypt, typically

---

[184] Jeremy Black and Anthony Green (1992) *Gods, Demons and Symbols of Ancient Mesopotamia: An Illustrated Dictionary*. Page 73-77

[185] S. Dalley (2000) *Myths from Mesopotamia: Creation, the Flood, Gilgamesh, and Others*, Page 164

dated to this period.

In *Nergal and Eresh-Kigal* the gods in the Heights were planning a feast, and as Eresh-Kigal was unable to leave the Underworld, they sent a messenger down to ask if she wanted to send someone to represent her at the feast. She decided to send her Minister Namtar, who then ascended the long staircase to the Heights to attend the feast. When Namtar arrived at the feast all the gods rose to show respect for the minister of Eresh-Kigal, all the gods except the brash young Nergal.

Nergal was summoned to the Underworld to answer for insulting the minister of Eresh-Kigal, and before he descended to the Underworld Ea, the Akkadian version of Enki, advised him to not eat the food of the Underworld, not to accept any gifts Eresh-Kigal might offer, and to not have sex with her. He didn't listen, and the two ended up making love for six days. On the sixth day, Nergal decided to return to the Heights, and sneaked off while Eresh-Kigal was still asleep, ascending the long staircase to the Heights without anyone seeing him.

When Eresh-Kigal woke up and found him missing, she went into a psychotic rant, and sent Minister Namtar up to the Heights to bring Nergal back down to the Underworld as she 'did not have enough delight with him before he left!' Namtar ascended the long staircase back up to the Heights, but could not find Nergal, and returned to the Underworld. This happened a few times before he finally found Nergal, and brought him back down to the Underworld for Eresh-Kigal to 'get more delight with.' In a later Babylonian version, Nergal returned on his own, and 'seized her by the hairdo, and pulled her from the throne,' following which he 'took some delight' from her. These two versions have been noted by Assyriologists as being part of a pattern of marginalization and privatization of goddesses[186] during the Akkadian, Babylonian, and Assyrian eras. After the two were reunited they made love for seven days, and Anu ordered his minister Kakka to go to Mount Nugi, and descend into Irkalla and tell Eresh-Kigal and Nergal that they were married.

Most of this story is odd, the idea that someone might be offer food, gifts, or sex, as a punishment for insulting the Queen of the Underworld, is odd. The fact that Nergal ran away and hid, suggests that this story parallels the Rape of Persephone from Greek mythology, but with the genders reversed. Nergal was even described as cringing while he was hiding from Minister Namtar, implying he was for some reason afraid of Eresh-Kigal. This story is completely incongruous with the general marginalization and pacification of female deities in the Akkadian and Babylonian eras and suggests that it dates to an earlier period. During her rant after finding out that Nergal had escaped the Underworld, Eresh-Kigal referred to herself as the Great Judge of the Underworld, which implies that she was the leader of the seven judges that had stopped Inanna from taking over Ganzir in *Inanna Descends into the Underworld.*

The fact that the ministers and Nergal could simply walk up and down a staircase to travel between

[186] Tikva Frymer-Kensky (1993) *In the Wake of the Goddesses: Women, Culture and the Biblical Transformation of Pagan Myth*

the Underworld and the Heights, portrays these as actual places, not the state of Death and Life, as Akkadian and Babylonian beliefs generally depicted Irkalla, the land of the dead. This matches the geography of the Dumuzid saga, where one could walk down from the Garden-of-the-Gods on top of a mountain, to Ganzir in a cave in the mountain. This geography is confirmed by Anu when he sends his minister Kakka to Mount Nugi, with orders to descend into the mountain to Irkalla to find Eresh-Kigal and Nergal. Mount Nugi is composed of the Sumerian logograms KUR, NU, and GI, which translate as 'Mountain of no return.' Which does match the Sumerian term 'land of no return,' the euphemism for Ganzir in the Dumuzid saga.

In the Sumerian era, Dumuzid wasn't the only husband of Inanna. According to the ancient records in the city of Kish, Zababa was married to Inanna from the earliest dynastic period.[187] As Zababa was identified as Inanna's husband in the 1st Kish Dynasty, he may be a Kish Civilization precursor to Dumuzid, although Dumuzid was not depicted as a war god or even a warrior. Zababa was a war-god, whose iconography included lions, implying the Guardians from the Garden-of-the-Gods, however, he was not depicted as a cherub or lion-man hybrid, he was depicted as a man with a lion or panther. If Zababa was a Guardian, then the Kishite story might have conflated the goddesses Inanna and Geshtinanna, as Geshtinanna married Amurru after Dumuzid's death,

---

[187] Jeremy Black and Anthony Green (1992) *Gods, Demons and Symbols of Ancient Mesopotamia: An Illustrated Dictionary*, Page 180-187

who seems to have been a Guardian.

In the Akkadian era, *Myth of Adapa and the South Wind*, Dumuzid and Gishzida were the two Guardians of the Gates of heaven. The Myth of Adapa, was originally recovered from a dig in Tel el-Amarna in Egypt, and typically dated to the archives of King Akhenaten, from circa 1350 BC. Additional copies have been recovered from the Library of Ashurbanipal of Assyria, from circa 650 BC, indicating that this tale was popular over a wide area, and for a very long time.

The story is about a priest of Ea (the Akkadian Enki), who was fishing in the Persian Gulf when a strong wind capsized his boat, and in a fit of rage, he cursed the South Wind to not blow for a week. Anu, the Akkadian version of An, called Adapa to heaven to account for his action, and Ea instructed him to gain the sympathy of Tammuz, the Akkadian Dumuzid, and Gishzida, the Akkadian Nin-Gishzida, the two guardians of the gates of heaven. Ea also told Adapa not to eat any of the food in heaven, because it was poisonous. When he got to the gates of heaven, the guardians offered him the food-of-life, and the water-of-life, which he refused, and when Anu later asked why he refused them, he stated that it was because Ea advised him to. This caused the gods to laugh, as Adapa had unknowingly refused immortality. Anu then cursed humanity with diseases because of Adapa's stopping the south wind from blowing. While the story is entertaining, it appears to be an Akkadian or Old Babylonian fiction, unrelated to the other myths of Dumuzid, and can clearly not be the inspiration for the Adonis, Attis, or Atunis cults across the Mediterranean.

Dumuzid is also mentioned in the Akkadian era *Epic of Gilgamesh* when Ishtar attempted to seduce Gilgamesh, and he rebuffed her advances by reminding her of how she treated Dumuzid. This version does match the Dumuzid saga, however, dates to much later and does not add any new information to the story. Many Akkadian and Babylonian stories were written that either added to the Dumuzid saga, or changed the connotations of the saga. In *The Most Bitter Cry*, the Underworld was described as a place where everything both 'exists' and 'does not exist,' implying an insubstantial existence.[188] Likewise in the Akkadian epic *In the Desert by the Early Grass* Dumuzid became a disembodied spirit in the Underworld and traveled around encountering other disembodied spirits.

These Akkadian era stories changed the narrative from something that could be interpreted in the mundane world, to something that was clearly supernatural. The bailiffs became demons. The judges became devils. Ganzir, which was originally described as a subterranean prison or gulag became the Netherworld, and the Queen of Kigal, became the Queen of the Dead. Likewise, the Garden-of-the-Gods became Heaven, another Netherworld, but with better food.

---

[188] Gregory Shushan (2009) *Conceptions of the Afterlife in Early Civilizations: Universalism, Constructivism, and near Death Experience*, Page 78

Adonis, Attis, Atunis, Tithonus, and Osiris

The story of Dumuzid being trapped in the underworld with Eresh-Kigal for half the year, and free to be with Inanna for half the year is clearly the basis of the Greek myth of Aphrodite and Adonis.[189] In the Greek myth Adonis ended up spending a third of the year in the Greek Underworld with Persephone, the Queen of the Underworld, and two-thirds of the year with Aphrodite. The earliest mention of Adonis that has survived is from the Greek poetess Sappho circa 600 BC, however, most of the surviving narrative of the story was added later by Greek and Roman writers.[190]

Various other cultures across the region had similar goddess-god duos with similar life-and-death annual cycles, including the Phrygian Cybele and Attis, whose cult can be traced back firmly to between 500 to 600 BC, thanks to a Phrygian rock-cut shrine dedicated to the 'Mother of the Mountain.'[191] In the Phrygian version of the story, Cybele was originally Agdistis and took the name Cybele after her male genitals were removed. A statue of a seated woman accompanied by lions has been recovered at Çatalhöyük, Turkey, and dates from 6000 BC, calling into question when the Cult of Cybele began, as it is ex-

---

[189] M. L. West (1997) *The East Face of Helicon: West Asiatic Elements in Greek Poetry and Myth*, Page 57
[190] Monica S. Cyrino (2010) *Aphrodite, Gods and Heroes of the Ancient World.* Page 95-97
[191] R. S. P. Beekes (2009) *Etymological Dictionary of Greek.* Page 794

actly how she was represented in the classical era.[192] Below is a depiction of Aphrodite and Adonis painted on a vase from circa 410 BC.

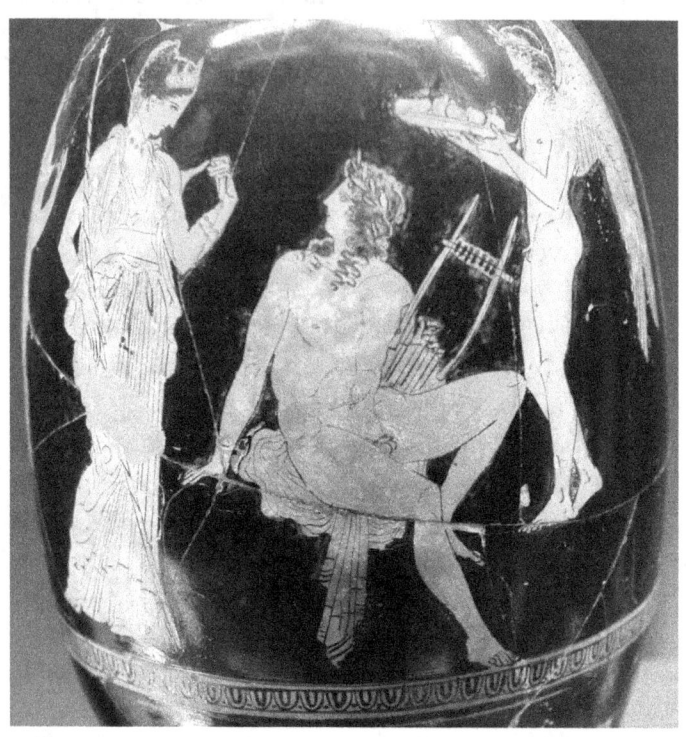

If one accepts that this is an 8000-year-old representation of Cybele, and thereby Inanna, one either has to accept the ULT of Mesopotamian history, in which Sumer was Ubaid, and existed since by at least 8000 BC, or that the Sumerians adopted a Phrygian deity into their pantheon, and put her right up at the

---

[192] S. A. Takács (1996) "Cybele, Attis and related cults," *Essays in memory of M.J. Vermaseren.* Page 376

top, with An, Enki, and Enlil, around 3000 BC in the CMT. On the opposite page are photos of three statues, a Roman-era statue of Cybele (left) from circa 50 AD, the Çatalhöyük Statuette (center) from circa 6000 BC, and an ancient statue of Cybele riding a lion (right) recovered from Roman-era ruins, but believed to predate Rome.

Significant similarities were noted between Dumuzid and Osiris in the early 1900s by anthropologist James Frazer. Both Dumuzid and Osiris were considered gods of the dead,[193] and were connected with grain,[194] and festival involving planting grains at the wrong time of the year, and were killed tragically, but then brought back to life by their wives, Inanna and Isis.[195] In both versions of the story, there is a special kind of food and water, in Sumer the food-of-life and water-of-life, in Egypt the food-of-

---

[193] John Gwyn Griffiths (1980) *The Origins of Osiris and His Cult*, Page 158-162, 185

[194] Tryggve N. D. Mettinger (2001) *The Riddle of Resurrection: "Dying and Rising Gods,"* Pages 15-18, 40-41

[195] Rosalie David (2002) *Religion and Magic in Ancient Egypt.* Page 157

the-gods and the water-of-the-gods.[196] Both Osiris and Dumuzid were also described as 'permanently youthful.'[197]

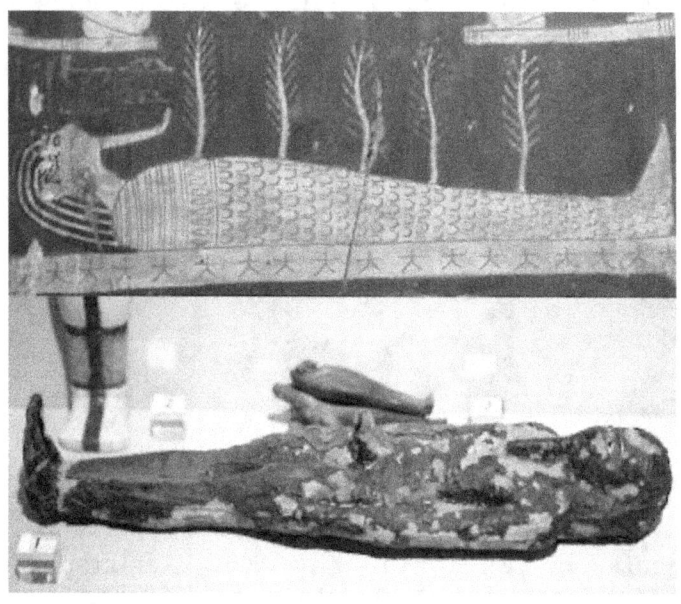

Above are photographs of an ancient Egyptian painting of Osiris' mummy sprouting grains, and a 'grain mummy.' Grain mummies were dried mud and seed statues, used in ancient Egypt to plant grain, likely to keep the Nile floods from washing the grain away. In mid-summer, grain mummies shaped like Osiris were used in a ceremony in which they were watered, sprouted, but then died as they

[196] Plutarch (c. 100 AD) *Isis and Osiris*, translated by Frank Cole Babitt (1936) Volume 5:39
[197] Donald B. Redford, editor (2003) *The Oxford Guide: Essential Guide to Egyptian Mythology*, Pages 302-307

weren't planted. This ceremony could have simply originated as a way to use up extra grain mummies or could be related to the similar festivals in Eurasia.

Egyptologists have debated the significance of these similarities, not just with Dumuzid, but with Tammuz, Adonis, and Attis, and have not come to a consensus.[198] The death of Osiris, along with his resurrection, his association with the grain sprouting ceremony, and his eternal youth date back to at least the Old Kingdom,[199] and many Egyptologists believe they may date back to the pre-dynastic era.[200]

If Osiris and Dumuzid do have a common ancestral story, it appears to have been very corrupted by one of the cultures during the early dynastic eras. This further complicates the issue for Assyriologists that would like to maintain the fiction that Dumuzid the Shepherd was a mythical version of Dumuzid the Fisherman, as Dumuzid the Fisherman lived during the time of the Egyptian Old Kingdom. Using the conventional timelines, the Old Kingdom was circa 2686 to 2181 BC, while the life of Dumuzid the Fisherman is guesstimated to be around 2600 BC.

If on the other hand the ULT is used, there is more than enough time for Dumuzid's story to have been corrupted into the Osiris myth, as the Inanna cult would have moved from Aratta to Uruk around the time that Lugal Banda became king, circa 9136 BC, while the Egyptian dynastic era would have be-

[198] Geraldine Pinch (2004) *Egyptian Mythology: A Guide to the Gods, Goddesses, and Traditions of Ancient Egypt.* Page 178-9
[199] John Gwyn Griffiths (1980) *The Origins of Osiris and His Cult.* Page 44
[200] Herman te Velde (1967) *Seth, God of Confusion.* Page 76-80

gun circa 5510 BC. The long-timeline also allows more than enough time for the Dumuzid story to have spread up to the Phrygians by 6000 BC when they made the statue of the 'Mother of the Mountain.' In the Etruscan version of the story, the heroes were Turan and Atunis. In this version, Turan was a beautiful young woman, and Atunis a beautiful young man, who were depicted as being in love. As the early Romans conquered and then assimilated the Etruscans, little else is known, other than their midsummer month was named after Turan, and she was sometimes depicted with wings, like Ishtar.[201]

The oldest Etruscan artwork depicting these heroes dates to only around 300 BC, meaning they could have been influenced by the Greek Aphrodite and Adonis. On the opposite page is a sketch of the back of an engraved Etruscan mirror from between 500 to 300 BC, which depicts Attis (left), Turan (center), and Zipunu (right).

---

[201] N. H. Ramage and A. Ramage (1996) *Roman Art, Upper Saddle River*, figure 1.39

179

Dionysus, Disonuso, Diwonijo, and Bacchus

The most enigmatic Greek god, Dionysus, was steeped in Dumuzid-Tammuz lore. For the Greeks, he was always the foreign god, even though being part of the Greek pantheon since the Mycenaean era, circa 1500 to 1100 BC, when they called him Disonuso.[202] This foreign god was also worshiped by the Minoans[203] under the name Diwonijo, although it is unclear when they started worshiping him.

The Minoans built a major civilization in the Aegean long before the Greeks. Their civilization was devastated by the volcanic eruption of Thera sometime between 1650 and 1500 BC, however, dating systems all disagree on when. Archaeologists working in Crete generally claim it was circa 1500 BC[204] due to the style of pottery being made at the time, carbon dating places it between 1627 and 1600 BC[205] by examining the remains of plants buried at the time. Egyptologists have found a layer of pumice they think is related to Thera at Tel el Dab'a that is dated to the reign of King Ahmose I, which places

---

[202] K. A. Raymoure (November 2, 2012) "Khania Linear B Transliterations" Minoan Linear A & Mycenaean Linear B. *Deaditerranean.*

[203] K. A. Raymoure (2014) "Possible evidence of human sacrifice at Minoan Chania," *Archaeology News Network*

[204] Barbara J. Sivertsen, (2009) "The Minoan Eruption," *The Parting of the Sea: How Volcanoes, Earthquakes, and Plagues Shaped the Story of the Exodus.* Page 25.

[205] Walter L. Friedrich, et al. (2006) "Santorini Eruption Radiocarbon Dated to 1627–1600 B.C." *American Association for the Advancement of Science.* 312 (5773): 548

the Thera eruption circa 1540 BC.[206] Meanwhile ice core samples from Greenland show evidence of a large volcanic eruption circa 1642 BC,[207] and dendrochronology shows a disruption of the normal growth cycles of trees circa 1628 BC in both North America[208] and Europe.[209] Additionally Chinese records of the year 1618 BC imply a large volcanic eruption somewhere in the northern hemisphere.[210]

On the opposite page is a photo of the ancient Greek painter Amasis' rendition of Dionysus, Demeter, and Persephone, from circa 525 BC. This eruption of Thera didn't destroy the Minoans but did cause a great deal of damage throughout the Aegean. The eruption caused tsunamis and ash-fall across the region damaging their economy and causing their civilization's decline. In the longer term, the decline of the Minoans ultimately allowed the rise of the Greeks. Like the history of other nearby cultures, the Minoans timeline is based on how it correlates with Egypt, however, unlike the Middle Eastern cultures, there is no complex written histories or invasions by other cultures before the Greeks invaded near the end of Minoan history.

---

[206] Louise Schofield (2007) *The Mycenaeans.* Page 69

[207] Bo M. Vinther, et al. (2006) "A synchronized dating of three Greenland ice cores throughout the Holocene," *Journal of Geophysical Research.* 111 (D13).

[208] M. G. L. Baillie (1989) "Irish Tree Rings and an Event in 1628 BC," *The Thera Foundation*

[209] H. Grudd, et al. (2000) "Swedish tree rings provide new evidence in support of a major, widespread environmental disruption in 1628 BC," *Geophysical Research Letters.* 27 (18): 2957-60

[210] K. P. Foster, et al. (1996) "Texts, Storms, and the Thera Eruption," *Journal of Near Eastern Studies.* 55 (1): 1-14

The Minoan timeline was largely the creation of Arthur Evans, circa 1900 AD. Evans was the discoverer of the Minoan civilization and subsequently divided the civilization into three periods which he lined up with the periods of the three Egyptian Kingdoms, based on imported Egyptian pottery and artifacts. Archaeologists working in Crete have largely followed Evans' model, adjusting the Minoan timeline to keep it in sync with the contemporary view of Egyptian history. This means the history is currently viewed as falling between 3500 and 1100 BC, beginning a few hundred years before the unification of Egypt, and ending during the Greek dark age. If Minoan history is placed in the ULT, then it would span approximately 6000 to 1100 BC.

Evans himself suggested that the earliest phase of Minoan civilization looked like an Egyptian Early Dynastic colony, predating the Old Kingdom in Egypt. Below is a photograph of the massive megalithic stones of the Gournia palace walls from the earliest phase of Minoan civilization, which looks like the masonry in the Egyptian megalithic temples and Osireion.

If Diwonijo was being worshiped throughout Minoan history, then he could plausibly be a direct precursor for Osiris, or he could have been adopted by the Minoans at some point from Osiris, however, there is no reason to assume he was. We have no stories surviving about Diwonijo or Disonuso, and are therefore limited to studying Dionysus and his Roman equivalent Bacchus, to understand this early Mediterranean version of Dumuzid. Unfortunately, as Dionysus was that mysterious 'foreign' god, he was tied to many cults, and there were many theories of his origin.

The Greeks tried to integrate him into their pantheon several ways and sometimes listed him as an Olympian. He was said to the son of Zeus and the mortal Seleme, or in the Orphic tradition the son of Zeus and Persephone, the Queen of the Underworld. In the Eleusinian mysteries, he was called Iacchus, the husband of Demeter. As Demeter was another deity inherited from the Minoans, who called her Damate,[211] and she was a mother-goddess, a grain-goddess,[212] and an earth-goddess, this shows a clear Minoan parallel to the Phrygian Cybele-Attis,[213] and the Cypriot Aphrodite-Adonis relationships.

The Eleusinian Mysteries was an ancient Greek religion that was practiced in the city of Eleusis. Little is known about the origin of the religion, however, it was practiced during the entire pre-Christian Greco-Roman era, in Greece and then Rome. It is believed to have originated somewhere in Anatolia or the Minoan Civilization. The name of the town, Eleu-

---

[211] Y. Duhoux (1994–1995) "LA > B da-ma-te = Déméter? Sur la langue du linéaire A," *Minos 29/30* (1994-1995): 289-294

[212] K. A. Raymoure (November 2, 2012) Inscription MY Oi 701. "si-to-po-ti-ni-ja". *Deaditerranean*

[213] Martin Nilsson (1967) *Die Geschichte der Griechische Religion.* Page 444

sis, is believed to be related to the Greek goddess Eileithyia, who was called Ereutija[214] during the Mycenaean era. This goddess was widely worshiped through the Aegean, under a variety of names including Elysia in Laconia and Messene.

Some have linked the name Elysia to the Greek concept of the island of the happy dead: the Elysian Fields.[215] The Elysian Fields, or Elysium, was a garden or land far to the west of Greece, described as a paradise without snow or storms. It was originally considered separate from the Underworld ruled by Hades and was where the gods went when they died. Later it became a place where anyone could go when they died, as long as the gods approved of the way they lived their life. Otherwise, they would be dragged to the fires of Hades' Underworld.

These two lands would later serve as the basis for the Christian heaven and hell concepts, neither of which have a basis in Judaism. In both classical and modern Judaism, the soul dies with the body, however, if deemed worthy will be resurrected at some point, when God gets around to it. Some exceptional Jews did get taken to heaven, such as Elijah and Enoch, however, they were alive when God took them, and were still alive when returned to the Earth. This understanding was clearly still present in the first group of Jewish Christians, as Jesus had to be resurrected before he could be taken up to heaven. However as Christianity spread across the Roman Empire, Heaven and Hades became the two

---

[214] K. A. Raymoure (November 2, 2012) "e-re-u-ti-ja," Minoan Linear A & Mycenaean Linear B. *Deaditerranean.*
[215] Hesiod (c. 700 BC) *Works and days.* 166ff.

fates waiting for everyone at the end of their lives.

In the Odyssey, circa 700 BC, Homer referred to the fair-haired Rhadamanthus ruling Elysium. Rhadamanthus' name is believed to be derived from the Greek word 'damázo' which means 'to overpower,' 'tame,' or 'conquer.' In the Greek legends of the ancient Minoan civilization, King Minos had a daughter named Ariadne, who was in charge of the labyrinth the Minotaur was kept in. In most versions of her story she married Dionysus,[216] however, according to Plutarch there was an alternate version of her story, where she was married to Rhadamanthus.[217] While we don't know what source Plutarch was using, he certainly would have known the more common Dionysus version, and so giving her this somewhat obscure husband seems odd unless he truly believed the Rhadamanthus version of the story was the original.

As both these gods were said to be married to Ariadne, and both were associated with the dead, it is plausible that these are two divergent versions of the Minoan Diwonijo. The story of Ariadne and Dionysus was certainly spread far enough that divergent version of Dionysus could have appeared, the Etruscans called them Areatha and Fufluns.[218]

The city of Eleusis was apparently originally called Saesara before Demeter visited the city, after which it was renamed Eleusis. This story does not make any sense unless the early Greeks considered

---

[216] Mary Renault (1962) *The Bull from the Sea*

[217] Plutarch (c. 100 AD) *Life of Theseus* 20

[218] Larissa Bonfante and Judith Swaddling (2006) *Etruscan Myths (The Legendary Past)*, Page 41, Figure 25

Eleusis to be another name for Demeter. The story of the city's renaming is embedded within the overarching narrative of the Eleusinian Mysteries. While Demeter was looking for her daughter Persephone and happened to be disguised as an old lady, she was found by the daughters of King Keleos of Saesara. They took her back to the palace to be the nursemaid to the baby Prince Demophoon. King Keleos' wife Queen Metaneira became jealous of the growing relationship between her son Demophoon and his nursemaid Demeter, and insulted Demeter, causing Demeter to remove her disguise, revealing herself to the Saesarian royal family. After that, King Keleos ordered the building of a shrine for Demeter in Saesara, and at some point the city's name was changed to Eleusis, to commemorate Demeter's visit.

On the opposite page is a diagram of an Etruscan engraved mirror back depicting a Satyr (left), Areatha (center-left), Fufluns (center-right), and Fufluns' mother Semla (right). It is unclear if this was ever a part of the mysteries, and seems like an unlikely chapter: 'Goddess stops in the middle of panicked quest to find daughter to nurse young prince.' This story is most likely something that was invented as theo-political propaganda, sometime in the Greek dark age, or, based on the archaic name, the earlier Mycenaean period.

Demeter's quest to rescue Persephone from the Underworld was a central theme of the Eleusinian Mysteries. In the Eleusinian Mysteries Persephone, who was also called Kore, meaning maiden in Greek, was abducted by Hades, ruler of the Underworld, which started Demeter's quest.

Demeter was so distraught over the loss of her daughter that she caused a drought, which caused both the god and mortals to starve. The people and gods cried out to Zeus, ruler of the Greek pantheon, and he decided to intercede, sending Hermes to the Underworld to demand that Hades release Persephone.

Hades obeyed Zeus' commands, but first tricked Persephone into eating some pomegranate seeds. Apparently, it was the law of the Fates, called Moirai in Greek, that once someone ate the fruit of the Underworld they were forced to live there eternally. This forced Persephone to spend four or six months in the Underworld each year. The accounts differ on the number of seeds she ate, and the resulting number of months in the Underworld. Below is a painting of Hades abducting Persephone, believed to have bee painted by the ancient Greek painter Nikomachos circa 345 BC.

These mysteries can be considered an elaborate story designed to explain why the seasons come and go, however, it is clearly related to the Dumuzid epic in several ways. Demeter and Inanna are both mother and earth goddesses. Persephone and Eresh-

Kigal were both the Queen of the Underworld. Both the Eleusinian Mysteries and the Sumerian epic *Inanna Descends to the Underworld* are focused on the tale of these two female protagonists, and not their husbands, Dionysus/Dumuzid or Gugalanna/Hades. In both cases when the god that interceded did so, he sent someone connected with sexual ambiguity down into the Underworld to do his bidding, Enki's gala priests, and Hermes, the father of Hermaphroditus, the hermaphrodite god.

There are obviously many differences too. In the Sumerian version, the woman that is forced to spend half the year in the Underworld is Geshtinanna, Inanna's sister-in-law, not the Queen of the underworld. In the Sumerian version, Gugalanna had died, and Eresh-Kigal was ruling the underworld, however, in the Eleusinian version Hades was alive and ruling the underworld. This point may indicate the Eleusinian version was drawn from a later Semitic version of the story where Nergal was co-ruling the Underworld with Eresh-Kigal.

The god that interceded was Zeus in the Eleusinian version, not An's equivalent Uranus, however, the Greeks really didn't have any interest in Uranus, and only some vague creation stories in which he was involved. However, Zeus' equivalent in the Sumerian pantheon was Enlil, Enki's Greek equivalent was Poseidon. The fact that the story was changed from Enki/Poseidon to Enlil/Zeus may date the adoption period.

Almost all of the gods in the story are found in the Mycenaean Greek period, Zeus as Diwe and

Diwo, Poseidon as Posedao or Posedawone, Demeter as Sitotptinija, Persephone as Preswa, and Dionysus as Diwonuso. The only god that does not seem to date back to the Mycenaean Greek period is Hades. Additionally, a couple of these gods can be traced back to Minoans, namely Dionysus as Diwonijo, and Demeter as Damate, meaning aspects of this story may date back to the Minoans, and were certainly known to the Mycenaean Greeks.

Zeus is an archetypal Indo-European storm-god, related to Indra, Thor, Jupiter, Perun, and many others. He was worshiped by the Mycenaean Greeks and is believed to have entered the Aegean region with the earliest Greeks by 1500 BC.[219] On the other hand, the origin of Poseidon's name has been debated since the time of ancient Greece and is theorized to be Pre-Greek,[220] inherited from the cultures in the Aegean before the Greeks migrated into the region.

What is clear is that in the Mycenaean period, Poseidon was far more popular than Zeus. Zeus gained popularity in the Greek Dark Ages, and emerged as the head of the Olympians, ruling Olympus and serving as the supreme god for the Greeks until the Christian era. Persephone's name is also believed to be Pre-Greek in origin as well, as ancient Greeks had several different versions of her name across their

---

[219] Oliver Dickinson (December 1999) "Invasion, Migration and the Shaft Graves," *Bulletin of the Institute of Classical Studies.* 43 (1): 97-107

[220] R. S. P. Beekes (2009) *Etymological Dictionary of Greek*, Page 337

territory.[221]

Hades name is of unknown origin. As with Poseidon and Persephone, Greeks argued the origin of Hades name through the classical period, and modern historians continue the debate. Plato devoted a section of his dialogue *Cratylus* to the etymology of Hades name, and modern linguists have proposed both Indo-European origins, and non-Greek origins. What is known is that in the time of Homer, circa 700 BC, he was known as Aides,[222] as well as other regional variations including Aidoneus (Ἀϊδωνεύς), Aidos (Ἀϊδος), Aidi (Ἀϊδι), and Aida (Ἀϊδα). Seeing the similarity between these names and the Cypriot Adonis is not difficult, however, Adonis was the youthful lover of Aphrodite, while Hades was the raper of Persephone, meaning that Hades could not be derived directly from Adonis.

The two gods could still both derive from contact with Phoenicians, as Adon simply meant 'lord' in Canaanite, and both were lords of something. In fact, both could be interpreted as Lords of the Dead, by the Canaanite era. Tammuz was the god that died for part of the year, and Nergal was married to the Queen of the Underworld. However, if Hades was an adaption of Adon it was clearly more corrupted than the Cypriot version. In the Greek version, it was Hades who raped the youthful Persephone, not the other way around, while in the Cypriot version Adonis was still the youthful lover of Aphrodite.

---

[221] Martin Nilsson (1967) *Die Geschichte der Griechische Religion.* Page 474

[222] Anatole Bailly (1963) " Ἀιδης" *Dictionnaire Grec - Français,* 26th Edition.

Gender role reversals aside, the correlations between the Rape of Persephone and Nergal and Eresh-Kigal, are difficult to ignore. In both cases, a youthful person is forced into a marriage by the ruler of the underworld. In one case the raper is the Queen of the Underworld, and in the other case, she becomes the Queen of the Underworld. In both Sumerian stories, the female characters are dominant, both Inanna and Eresh-Kigal are depicted as being both generally and sexually dominant in their relationships with their respective husbands. The Greek Aphrodite and Demeter goddesses were similarly depicted, as was the Phrygian Cybele, however, Persephone was the opposite, an adolescent girl abducted by Hades.

While many of the western stories of Aphrodite, Demeter, and Cybele might be based on adopted beliefs dating from the Sumerian period, the Rape of Persephone must have been inspired by the later subservient Eresh-Kigal from the Babylonian period. The Babylonian era version of *Nergal and Eresh-Kigal* is known to date to at least 1350 BC, and has been found as far west as Egypt, and so it is plausible that it could be the source for the Greek story.

The ancient Greeks themselves debated where the foreign god Dionysus had come from. In some Greek cults Dionysus was considered a Thracian and Phrygian god,[223] in others he was Asian, and in others he was Ethiopian. The Greek historian Pliny the El-

---

[223] Thomas McEvilley (2002) *The Shape of Ancient Thought.* Pages 118-121

der,[224] and the Roman historian Arrian,[225] both claimed the Dionysus had originated in India, Pliny claiming that he had founded the first Indian dynasty 6451 years before the conquest of Alexander. The ancient Greeks believed Dionysus' name was derived from the Greek words 'dios' and 'nysa.' Dios meant 'Zeus' and implied 'god' when embedded in the name of another god.[226] Nysa referred to the name of the mountain Dionysus was born on, and where he lived with the Nysiads.[227]

Unfortunately, the Greeks didn't know where Mount Nysa was. Hesychius of Alexandria, who lived around 500 AD, listed a number of locations that different ancient Greeks had suggested for Mount Nysa including Arabia, Babylon, Cilicia, Egypt, Ethiopia, India, Libya, Lydia, Macedonia, Naxos, the Red Sea, Syria, Thessaly, and Thrace. The Greeks that preferred the Indian origin, believed that Mount Nysa, was Mount Meru. Nysa becomes even more complicated than simply being a long lost mountain, with Pherecydes of Syros observation in the 6th century BC, that Nysa was derived from 'nusa' an archaic Greek word for 'tree.' These correlations with other Eurasian belief systems have led many scholars to associate Nysa with the axis-mundi world-mountain or world-tree concept.[228]

Dionysus and Demeter, as Diwonijo and Damate, are both Minoan gods that the earliest Greeks either

---

[224] Pliny the Elder (79 AD) *Naturalis Historia*, 6.59-60
[225] Arrian of Nicomedia (c. 150 AD) *Indica*, 9.9
[226] Michael Janda (2010) *Die Musik nach dem Chaos*. Pages 16-44
[227] Homer (c. 750 BC) Hymn 26 to *Dionysus*. 2 ff
[228] Michael Janda (2010) *Die Musik nach dem Chaos*. Pages 16-44

adopted or synchronized with their existing gods. This means that the Dumuzid and Inanna or Tammuz and Ishtar story could have been adopted by the Minoans at any point in their history. As both Poseidon and Persephone are believed to be pre-Greek names as well, the core cast of characters from the Dumuzid tale are all present: Dumuzid and his wife Inanna, her sister/daughter Persephone, and Poseidon, the god that intercedes. Without Hades, Persephone could not have been raped, and so had to be the Queen of the Underworld in her own right.

The Greeks inherited some odd stories from the Minoans, including one about the birth and death of Zeus in a cave on Crete. As Zeus is an Indo-European deity, and the Minoans are generally not considered to have been Indo-Europeans, this must have originally been a different god that became conflated with Zeus at some point after the Greeks arrived in the Aegean. This Zeus was known by the name Zeus Velchanos, and is said to have been born, and then later died, in Dictaean cave, today identified as Psychro Cave.[229] Zeus Velchanos was always depicted as a youth and was married to a great goddess in the Minoan religion, although it isn't clear which one.

Throughout Greek history Hades was commonly called Zeus by those wishing to avoid saying the name Hades, generally titled as Zeus Chthonios, Zeus Katachthonios, or Zeus Plousios. All of these Zeuses' titles referred to the abode of Hades. Clearly, the Greeks were using the word 'Zeus' as a synonym for 'god,' meaning Zeus Chthonios can be translated

---

[229] William Smith, editor (1873) *A Dictionary of Greek and Roman biography and mythology*

as 'Earthly god', Zeus Katachthonios means 'god under the Earth,' and Zeus Plousios means 'god bringing wealth.' If the Classical Greeks used the name Zeus when referring to Hades, it is plausible that Zeus Velchanos may have been the Minoan forerunner of Hades, married to the Queen of the Underworld, but still a youth, like the Babylonian Nergal.

This would imply that the big shift in the beliefs began sometime during the early Greek era when the sky-father god was interjected into the story, and Persephone went from being the Queen of the Underworld to a rape victim. In the Greek story about the rape of Persephone, it is, in fact, Zeus that advised Hades to abduct Persephone and rape her. In this context, this version of the story seems like a deliberate attack on the ancient goddesses of the region. Zeus not only had the Queen of the Underworld abducted and raped, but he also got to play the hero when the Earth-mother came crying and begging for the release of Persephone. A trifecta of theo-propaganda, in which the sky-father subjugated both of the ancient goddesses and got to play the compassionate hero who frees the maiden.

In the Eleusinian version of Dionysus, he was sometimes called Iacchus, although historians do not know why as the Eleusinian Mysteries were never written down. This name seems to be the source of the name of Bacchus, the Roman version of Dionysus.

Both the Greek and Roman versions of this god's worship were focused on the drinking of a psychoactive wine that would put participants into an altered state of consciousness. After the Cult of Bacchus had spread to Rome circa 200 BC additional aspects were introduced, including ripping apart living animals and eating them raw, and poly-amorous orgies. In 186 BC[230] the Senate issued the legislation to reform the Bacchanalia, placing the priests of the cult under imperial authority. According to the Roman historian Livy writing 200 years later, the Senate needed to execute 7000 cult leaders to exert their authority over the Cult of Bacchus. Over the following two centuries Bacchus merged with the Roman god of wine Liber Pater.

---

[230] Basilio Perri (17 February 2014) *The so called Senatus Consultum de Bacchanalibus detailed analysis of the language.* Pages 3-.

The Greeks also incorporated the story of Eos and Tithonus into their pantheon, pictured above on a Greek vase from circa 470 BC. Eos and Tothonus appear to be an Anatolian version of the story, adopted during the Greek dark ages or earlier. Eos was the Titaness of the dawn, descended from a Proto-Indo-European archetype called Hausos. Other goddesses derived from Hausos include the Vedic goddess Ushas, Baltic goddess Aušrinė, and Roman goddess Aurora. Eos' young lover was Tithonus, a prince of Troy long before the Battle of Troy. In Homer's version of the myth, Eos fell in love with Tithonus, and asked Zeus to grant him immortality, which Zeus did, however, she did not ask Zeus to keep Tithonus young, and so he aged but could not die. As described in the Hymn to Aphrodite:

> 'but when loathsome old age pressed full upon him, and he could not move nor lift his limbs, this seemed to her in her heart the best counsel: she laid him in a room and put to the shining doors. There he babbles endlessly, and no more has strength at all, such as once he had in his supple limbs.'[231]

This darker version of the story takes a different path from most, in which the Dumuzid character either remained eternally young or periodically died and resurrected, also remaining young. The core of this story does appear to derive from the ancient story, of an older more powerful female monarch or goddess, and her younger male spouse who was granted immortality. The fact that the Titaness was an Indo-European goddess implies that the Greeks

---

[231] Unknown Author (c 650 BC) *Homeric Hymn to Aphrodite*, 218 ff

may have carried the story into Greece, however the fact that they placed the hero in Troy, also indicates a possible Anatolian source for the story. Either way, this version appears to be Indo-European in origin.

Panthers and Lions

There is a common element across the varied Dumuzid-like myths: panthers and lions. These are not the panthers of today's world, but rather an extinct species that once apparently lived on the Mountain in the Steppes. The modern word panther is derived from the name of the mythical creature. According to Pliny the Elder, panthers emitted a scent that drew other animals to them, which they would then kill.[232] This sounds like an attempt to explain the strange behavior of animals infected by toxoplasma, which is a parasite most felines carry. When infected by toxoplasma most animals lose there natural fear of felines, some even become attracted to their natural predators. In the middle ages, the dragon was added to the panther myth as the only creature immune to the panther's scent.

In the Greek myths of Dionysus, he rode a panther. Which is virtually identical to Pravati riding her mounts Dawon the lion and Manasthala the tiger. Parvati, whose name means 'mountain' has been described as the Indian version of Cybele[233] and Aphrodite.[234] On the next page is a photograph of a Greek painting from circa 370 BC of Dionysus riding a Panther (center). Dionysus' Roman equivalent Bachhus rode a chariot pulled by a panther. Likewise, the chariots of Ishtar,[235] Cybele, Demeter, and another variant Rhea, were all pulled by lions.

---

[232] Pliny the Elder (79 AD) *Natural History*, Book 8, 23
[233] Edward Balfour (1885) "Parvati" *The Cyclopaedia of India and of Eastern and Southern Asia*, Page 153
[234] Edmund Ronald Leach (2001) *The Essential Edmund Leach: Culture and human nature*, Page 85
[235] Jana Garai (1973) *The Book of Symbols*

Inanna was depicted as standing on the back of lions, implying she rode them. In all the Mesopotamian depictions the lions were depicted as having no manes, which led to Greeks identifying them as panthers. Dumuzid's alter-ego Ishtaran was also depicted as being accompanied by lions, as was Zababa. These panthers or lions were sometimes also given the power of human speech and the ability to use tools, in the myths surrounding them, becoming the lion-man Guardians in the Garden-of-the-Gods in the Dumuzid saga.

This motif is also found in Egypt, where the lion-woman hybrid Sekhmet was the consort of Ptah. The Egyptian 'Fortress of the Smiths,' Memphis, was named after Ptah, which connects Semhket back with the Sumerian story of a garden in a Fortress of

Smiths on a mountain in the steppes. She even had a partner guardian, Bastet, who was also still depicted as a fierce lion-woman in the Old Kingdom, however, she became a housecat-woman hybrid by the New Kingdom.[236] Below is a photograph of a Hindu statue of Pravati riding her mount Dawon.

---

[236] Geraldine Pinch (2002) *Egyptian Mythology: A Guide to the Gods, Goddesses, and Traditions of Ancient Egypt*, Page 115

This twin lion Guardian concept has been in China, since at least the Han Dynasty. Guardian Lions, also called lion-dogs have been common at the entrances to important buildings, such as temples and palaces throughout China. These Guardian Lions are believed to have been imported to China from India by Buddhist missionaries around 2000 years ago. Due to Chinese cultural influence over the past two thousand years, the Guardian Lions are now commonly seen in Cambodia, Japan, Korea, Laos, Myanmar, Nepal, Singapore, Sri Lanka, Thailand, Vietnam. Below is a photograph of a Lion Guardian in the Forbidden City, Beijing.

While the anthropomorphic lion-people may be more entertaining, the fact that there are often the depictions of gods with lions or panthers suggests that the Guardians may have originally been lion-tamers and not human-feline hybrids. Preposterous as riding a large cat might seem, the Panther myth explains the lion-men chimeras connected to the Dumuzid lore stories across several cultures.

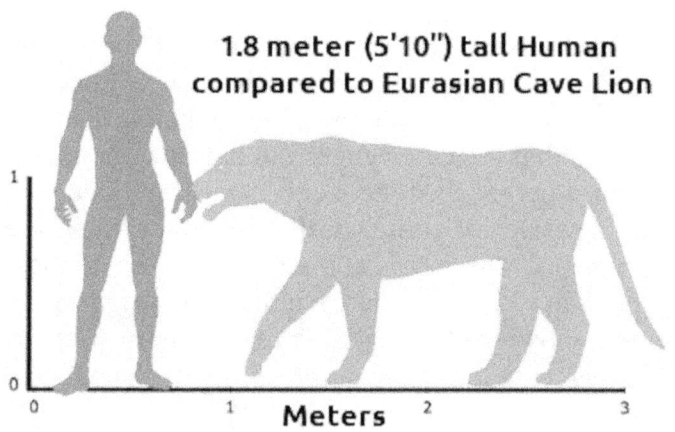

1.8 meter (5'10") tall Human compared to Eurasian Cave Lion

Several extinct large cats once roamed the Eurasian continent, whether humans ever tamed or rode them is a different question. Saber-toothed cats and European Leopards became extinct around 27,000 to 28,000 years ago,[237] while the Eurasian cave lions became extinct circa 10,900 years ago.[238] The European leopards would have been virtually identical to the leopards that currently roam Africa and Southern Asia, which are slightly smaller than humans, and therefore could not serve as a mount,

---

[237] Jelle W. F. Reumer, et al. (2003) "Late Pleistocene survival of the saber-toothed cat Homotheriumin northwestern Europe," *Journal of Vertebrate Paleontology.* 23: 260

[238] R. Barnett, et al. (2009) "Phylogeography of lions (Panthera leo ssp.) reveals three distinct taxa and a late Pleistocene reduction in genetic diversity," *Molecular Ecology.* 18 (8): 1668-1677

however, have been successfully raised in captivity, and can be trained to some extent. Saber-toothed cats were slightly larger than leopards, however still not large enough to ride. If any were ever tamed it is unlikely to ever be known.

The Eurasian cave lions were one of the largest felines we know of and were the size of the first horses humans rode. They also match the Panther myth in that they are believed to have had no mane. As for whether they were ever tamed or ridden we may never know, however, if the Panther myth of a rideable cat was based on a real animal, it was most likely a Eurasian cave lion. On the previous page is a graph showing the relative size of a human and a Eurasian cave lion.

Yemo the Shepherd

Another archaic hero that has major correlations with King Dumuzid the Shepherd is the reconstructed Indo-European hero Yemo the founder twin. Yemo has been reconstructed as part of the Indo-European pantheon based on several similar heroes found in ancient Indo-European beliefs. These include the Hindu god Yama, the Zoroastrian King Jamshid, and the Germanic ice-giant Ymir.

The Zoroastrian and Hindu versions seem to preserve more of the original story, as the Indo-Iranian peoples became literate long before the Germanic tribes. The oldest Germanic poems that mention Ymir only date to the early 1200s AD. Meanwhile, Yama is first mentioned in Mandala 10 of the Rig Veda Samhita, which the conventional Indian timeline (CIT) dates to circa 1500 to 1200 BC. The Zoroastrian King Jamshid was first mentioned in Yasht 19, Vendidad 2, of the Avesta, where he was named Yima-Kshaeta in the Younger Avestan language. The Vendidad, and the Young Avestan sections of the Avesta, were likely compiled in Central Asia, sometime between 3700 and 900 BC, although there is a great deal of debate about the dating of the Avesta.

In the somewhat confusing Avestan story of Yima, he began life as a shepherd, yet is also listed as the fourth king of the Pishdadian Dynasty. This dynasty preceded the Kayanian dynasty, who were apparently in power when the Avesta was compiled, however, no physical evidence of either dynasty has been found. While he was out shepherding, he was approached by a being of light called Ahura Mazda, who asked Yima to teach his law to the people. Yima refused, and they negotiated a deal where Yima agreed to rule over and nourish the earth and make sure that living things prospered. In trade for being a good king, Ahura Mazda gave Yima a dagger, a golden seal, and immortality for all his people.

After three hundred years had passed, the land that Yima's people inhabited was full. This land was called Airyanem Vaejah, and its inhabitants were the Aryans, outside of it was the lands of the daevas who served Ahriman. After three hundred years, Ahura Mazda returned to Yima and told him that the land was overpopulated, and so King Yima took the dagger and the golden seal and expanded the land of the Airyanem Vaejah. All of this is interpreted some-what magically in the Zoroastrian religion, wherein the daevas are insubstantial demons, and Ahriman is the devil, however, the story itself seems somewhat ordinary other than the immortality, and beings of light that kept visiting the ancient Aryans.

The expanded Airyanem Vaejah was able to house the Aryans for six centuries before it became overpopulated again. And so once more King Yima took his dagger and his golden seal and expanded the Airyanem Vaejah. Again the expanded Airyanem Vaejah was able to house the Aryans for some time, but then began getting overpopulated around 900 years later, and so once more King Yima expanded the land. Soon afterward Ahura Mazda returned, with a contingent of yazatas, a word that is generally translated as angels. King Yima also brought along a council of immortal Aryans when meeting with Ahura Mazda. The beings of light warned the king and his council of immortals of the coming evil winters. Apparently, somewhere outside of the Airyanem Vaejah, Ahriman had done something that was causing the world's climate to change. Ahura Mazda warned Yima before the onset of the evil winters, and advised him to build an underground city described in the Vendidad 2:22-30:

22 'And Ahura Mazda spake unto Yima, saying: 'O fair Yima, son of Vivanghat! Upon the material world the evil winters are about to fall, that shall bring the fierce, deadly frost; upon the material world the evil winters are about to fall, that shall make snow-flakes fall thick, even an aredvi [fourteen fingers] deep on the highest tops of mountains.'

23 'And the beasts that live in the wilderness, and those that live on the tops of the mountains, and those that live in the bosom of the dale shall take shelter in underground abodes.'

24 'Before that winter, the country would bear plenty of grass for cattle, before the waters had flooded it. Now after the melting of the snow, O Yima, a place wherein the footprint of a sheep may be seen will be a wonder in the world.'

25 'Therefore make thee a Vara, long as a riding-ground [2 miles] on every side of the square, and thither bring the seeds of sheep and oxen, of men, of dogs, of birds, and of red blazing fires. Therefore make thee a Vara, long as a riding-ground on every side of the square, to be an abode for man; a Vara, long as a riding-ground on every side of the square, for oxen and sheep.'

26 'There thou shalt make waters flow in a

bed a hathra [1 mile] long; there thou shalt settle birds, on the green that never fades, with food that never fails. There thou shalt establish dwelling-places, consisting of a house with a balcony, a courtyard, and as gallery.'

27 'Thither thou shalt bring the seeds of men and women, of the greatest, best, and finest on this earth; thither thou shalt bring the seeds of every kind of cattle, of the greatest, best, and finest on this earth.'

28 'Thither thou shalt bring the seeds of every kind of tree, of the highest of size and sweetest of odour on this earth; thither thou shalt bring the seeds of every kind of fruit, the best of savour and sweetest of odour. All those seeds shalt thou bring, two of every kind, to be kept inexhaustible there, so long as those men shall stay in the Vara.'

29 'There shall be no humpbacked, none bulged forward there; no impotent, no lunatic; no malicious, no liar; no one spiteful, none jealous; no one with decayed tooth, no leprous to be pent up, nor any of the brands wherewith Angra Mainyu stamps the bodies of mortals.'

30 'In the largest part of the place thou shalt make nine streets, six in the middle part, three in the smallest. To the streets of the largest part thou shalt bring a thousand seeds of men and women; to the streets of the middle part, six hundred; to the streets of the smallest part, three hundred. That Vara thou shalt seal up with thy golden seal, and thou shalt make a door, and a window self-shining within."

The *Vendidad* continues with King Yima building the described underground city, and then taking two thousand Aryans into the Vara and sealing the door before the evil winters covered the Airyanem Vaejah with snow covering the valleys as high as the peaks of the mountains. There are certainly some differences between this version of the story and many of the other Dumuzid like stories. For one, there are no female deities present. This is however due to the nature of the Avesta itself. Zarathustra was teaching a monotheistic religion, and therefore all gods, other than Ahura Mazda, were demoted to either yazatas or daevas. There are however several similarities to the Dumuzid stories. Both kings are also called 'the Shepherd,' both stories include an underground city, both stories involve immortality, and most distinctively, both stories are set at the onset of the Last Glacial Period. According to the Sumerian King List Dumuzid's reign was somewhere between 129,579 and 93,579 BC, while the Last Glacial Period is estimated to have begun 115,000 years ago.

Considering that both the Avestan Yima and Greek Tithonus descend from a Proto-Indo-European original, it seems that the followers of Zarathustra cut a lot from the story, including Eos, and possibly something going wrong with whatever immortality process Zeus/Ahura Mazda gave the Aryans. While the two stories are greatly divergent, the final resting place of both deities seems to be similar. The room where Eos left Tithonus was sealed with shining doors, while the Vara, which Yima never left, was described as being closed with a golden seal, which also turned on the 'self-shining window,' which has historically been interpreted as either a magical or an artificial light source, depending on the interpreter.

The Queen of Heaven

Throughout the Babylonian Dark Age, the worship of Inanna spread throughout the Semitic cultures of Mesopotamia under a variety of local names, including the Babylonian and Assyrian Ishtar, Canaanite Astarte, and Hebrew Asherah, as well as north into the Hittite civilization under the name of Aserdu. She was also known under the titles of Elat, meaning 'goddess,' and Qodesh, meaning 'holiness.' During the Second Egyptian Dark Age worship of the goddess spread into Egypt under the name of Qetesh, which was carried into Egypt by Canaanites starting in the 14th Dynasty. Below is a photo of a Sumerian-era seal impression depicting Inanna riding a lion.

This strongly implies that the Babylonian Dark Age happened before the 14th Dynasty, however, that is not the conventional view. Currently, the 14th Dynasty is placed between 1705 and 1690 BC

CET, while the Babylonian Dark Age is placed between the fall of the Old Hittite Kingdom circa 1524 BC CET, and the foundation of the Middle Assyrian and New Hittite Kingdoms sometime before the Battle of Megiddo in 1457 BC. In the ULT the two dark ages happened at the same time, with the 14th Dynasty happening between 2793 and 2533 BC, while the Babylonian Dark Age happened between 2965 BC and sometime before the Battle of Megiddo circa 1457 BC.

The holy city of this goddess was the city of Kadesh, also transliterated as Qadesh, located near the modern border of Syria and Lebanon. The earliest reference to this city is from the reign of King Ishi-Addu of Qatna, who was contemporary with the Assyrian Old Kingdom King Shamshi-Adad I, from circa 3158 to 3191 BC ULT (1785 to 1752 BC CMT). It is unclear when the city was renamed Kadesh, however, the older Akkadian name was recorded as Gizza.[239] The name was clearly named Kadesh at the end of the dark age as the King of Kadesh led two resistance movements against Egyptian expansion, culminating in the Battle of Megiddo in 1457 BC, which led to the collapse of the Mitanni Empire, and the Battle of Kadesh in 1274 BC, which led to the collapse of the Hittite Empire.

In each culture, this goddess was known as the 'Queen of Heaven,' which is a clear descendant of Inanna's title 'Lady of Heaven.' In each culture, this Queen of Heaven was also married to the local highest god outside of Babylonia and Assyria where she was married to Tammuz. In Canaan she was married

---

[239] A. B. Lloyd (1993) *Herodotus*, Page 162

to El, in Israel she was married to Yahweh, in the Hittite Empire she was married to Elkunirsa, and in Egypt, she was married to Ptah. Below is a photograph of a New Kingdom relief of Qetesh riding a lion (center), accompanied by Ptah (left).

According to the Phoenician Historian Sanchuniathon's *Phoenician History* from the Egyptian New Kingdom era, the Canaanite Astarte was also the Greek Titaness Dione, whose name also translates as 'goddess.'[240] Dione appears to have been worshiped

---

[240] Saul M. Olyan (1988) *Asherah and the cult of Yahweh in Is-*

in the Mycenaean era under then name Di-u-ja in the Linear-B script. In *Phoenician History*, Dione was married to El, who the Greeks considered the Canaanite version of the Titan Cronos. This suggests that in the Mycenean pantheon Cronos' wife was Dione. In the later Greek pantheon of the Classical era, Cronus' wife was Rhea, an Earth and nature goddess, who was also depicted as riding a lion. Below is a photo of a Greek painting of Rhea riding a lion from circa 450 BC.

The Mycenean Greek civilization is generally dated to between 1600 and 1100 BC, however, some archaeologists have suggested the early Greeks may have been in Greece since 2500 BC or earlier. The Myceneans appeared in Greece during the Second Egyptian Dark Age and Babylonian Dark Age, showing up in the records of the New Hittite and New Egyptian Empires as a significant power from the beginning of the New Kingdom era. The Egyptians referred to the Greeks as Danaya, starting circa 14 37 BC, during the reign of King Thutmose the third early in the New Kingdom era. The Hittites called the Greeks the Ahhiyawa, a reference to Achaea, in Greece, starting around 1400 BC as the New Kingdom emerged from the Babylonian Dark Age.

The fact that the worship of the Queen of Heaven spread as far as it did, integrating into many local religions during this dark age speaks volumes as to how long the dark age lasted. These Queens of Heaven and their respective husbands formed a widespread belief system throughout the Middle East, Egypt, and the Aegean, in which the lion-riding Queen of Heaven was married to the supreme god in each region, often supplanting older goddesses. The fact that Inanna's cult was limited to the Temples in Uruk and Nippur before the Akkadian era, and only started expanding in the Old Babylonian era, is well documented by Assyriologists.[241]

In the conventional timelines, the worship of Inanna the Queen of Heaven started spreading from Uruk circa 2334 BC during the rule of Sargon of

---

[241] Gwendolyn Leick (1998) *A Dictionary of Ancient Near Eastern Mythology*, Page 86-87

Akkad. During the Old Babylonian Empire, between 1894 and 1595 BC, the worship of Ishtar the Queen of Heaven became widely practiced in Babylonia, where she was married to Tammuz. The worship of Astarte the Queen of Heaven spread to Canaan likely before 1752 BC, where she became the patron goddess of Kadesh as the wife of El. In Canaan, she was also known as Qodesh, which is the name that the Canaanite 14th Dynasty used when they introduced her worship to Egypt. Even though the Canaanite 14th Dynasty was only 15 years long, Qetesh became widely worshiped across Egypt as Ptah's wife, replacing Ptah's original consorts Bastet and Sekhmet.

Sometime during the Old Hittite Empire, between 1664 and 1524 BC Aserdu was adopted by the Hittites, as the wife of Elkunirsa. Elkunirsa's name literally translates as 'El the Creator of Earth,'[242] implying the Hittites had adopted El along with Astarte from the Canaanites. Sometime before 1437 BC, the Mycenaean Greeks adopted Elat into their pantheon as Dione and had her married to the Titan Cronos. This timeline is possible but does not seem likely given how quickly certain events needed to take place, such as the Egyptians accepting Qetesh as Ptah's wife in only 15 years.

In the ULT, the worship of the Inanna the Queen of Heaven started spreading from Uruk circa 3885 BC during the rule of Sargon of Akkad. During the Old Babylonian Empire, between 3352 and 3038 BC, the worship of Ishtar the Queen of Heaven became

---

[242] Herbert Donner and Wolfgang Röllig (1962-1964) *Kanaanäische und aramäische Inschriften.*

widely practiced in Babylonia, where she was married to Tammuz. The worship of Astarte the Queen of Heaven spread to Canaan likely before 3191 BC, where she became the patron goddess of Kadesh as the wife of El. In Canaan, she was also known as Qodesh, which is the name that the Canaanite 14th Dynasty used when they introduced her worship to Egypt. During the 260-year-long Canaanite 14th Dynasty, Qetesh became widely worshiped across Egypt as Ptah's wife, replacing Ptah's original consorts Bastet and Sekhmet. Sometime during the Old Hittite Empire, between 3103 and 2965 BC, Aserdu and Elkunirsa were adopted by the Hittites, from the Canaanites. Sometime before 1437 BC, the Mycenaean Greeks adopted Elat into their pantheon as Dione and had her married to the Titan Cronos. The longer timeline of the ULT does seem to make more sense than the conventional timelines, as religions generally take centuries to become adopted by large portions of a nation's population.

Antediluvian Eridu

The first two kings listed on the Sumerian King Lists were Alulim and Alalngar who were listed as the kings of the antediluvian Eridu, between 266,379 to 237,579 BC and 237,579 to 201,579 BC respectively. This time period falls within a highly variable time in the Earth's climatic history. According to the analysis of ice-core samples from Antarctica, around 270,000 years ago, the world was in a glacial period. By 240,000 years ago the world had emerged from that glacial period, however, it sank back to a glacial period within 10,000 years, and then rose back out of that glacial period within another 10,000 years. The world remained in this state until around 200,000 years ago when the world sank into the Penultimate Glacial Period. Below is a graph showing the analysis of ice core samples from the European Project for Ice Coring in Antarctica (EPICA) and the Russian Vostok Station, covering the last 750,000 years.

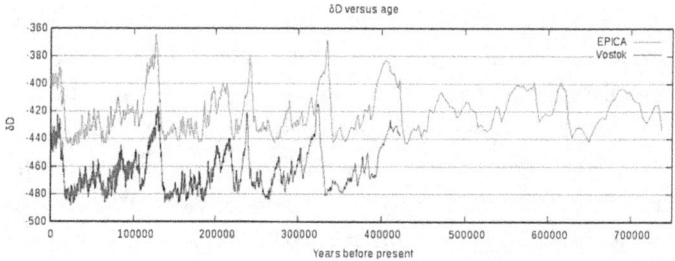

This rapidly fluctuating time period falls within one of the most chaotic periods of the last 800,000 years. The foundation of Eridu at circa 266,379 BC, roughly correlates with the depth of the glacial period of the era circa 270,000 years ago. The transition from Alulim to Alalngar at circa 237,579 BC, roughly corresponds to the height of the brief inter-glacial around 240,000 years ago. And finally, the fall of Eridu circa 201,579 BC, happened around the beginning of the Penultimate Glacial Period circa 200,000 years ago.

The name Eridu is generally translated as 'mighty place' or 'guidance place,' depending on the translator. The Sumerian logograms that spell out Eridu are NUN and KI. Like many Sumerian words, the logograms do not spell out the pronunciation of the word, meaning that the word was either adopted or inherited from another culture. These logograms can be translated as:

NUN: prince, noble, master, to rise up, great, fine, deep

KI: earth, place, area, location, ground, grain

This would mean that Eridu's original name could be translated as something vague like 'prince of the area,' or 'noble place,' or, conversely, as something specific, like 'Prince of Grain,' which is similar to the mythical Chinese King Hou Ji, whose name translates as 'Lord of Millet.' The origin of millet is a significant historical enigma, as the grain appears to have originated in multiple places on the Earth. In China the cultivation of foxtail-millet and broom-corn-millet has been traced back to between 21,000 to 17,500 BC,[243] while proso-millet was domesticated

---

[243] Li Liu (2015) "A Long Process Towards Agriculture in the Middle Yellow River Valley, China: Evidence from Macro-and Micro-Botanical Remains," *Journal of Indo-Pacific Archaeology*

in Greece sometime before 3000 BC.[244] Little-millet was domesticated in South Asia by 3000 BC. Pearl-millet was domesticated in Mali by 2500 BC,[245] and finger-millet was domesticated in Ethiopia sometime before 2000 BC.[246] The cultivation of Asian varieties of millet had spread across the Eurasian steppes to Europe by 5000 BC,[247] while both East and West African varieties of millet had spread to India by 1800 BC.[248] Foxtail-millet (priyangu), barnyard-millet (anu) and black-finger-millet (syamaka) are all mentioned in the Yajur-Veda,[249] indicating that they were all being cultivated in Central Asia by 1800 BC ULT (1200 CIT).

The wide-spread range of wild millet varieties has been debated among palaeoethnobotanists, questioning whether the wide-spread range represents the wild progenitor of millet or represents feral forms of millet that escaped from domesticated production.[250]

35 (2015): 3-14

[244] Mark Nesbitt, et al. (January 1988) "Some Recent Discoveries of Millet (Panicum miliaceum L. and Setaria italica (L.) P. Beauv.) at Excavations in Turkey and Iran," *Anatolian Studies* (38): 85-97

[245] Katie Manning, et al. (2011) "4500-Year old domesticated pearl millet (Pennisetum glaucum) from the Tilemsi Valley, Mali: new insights into an alternative cereal domestication pathway," *Journal of Archaeological Science.* 38: 312-32

[246] J. M. M. Engels, et al. (1991) *Plant Genetic Resources of Ethiopia*

[247] A. Lawler (2009) "Bridging East and West: Millet on the move," *Science.* 325: 942-943

[248] J. M. M. Engels, et al. (1991) *Plant Genetic Resources of Ethiopia*

[249] Mira Roy (2009) "Agriculture in the Vedic Period," *Indian Journal of History of Science*, 44 (4): 497-520

[250] Daniel Zohary and Maria Hopf (2000) *Domestication of*

While there is currently no known evidence for the cultivation of millet prior to Chinese adoption circa 21,000 BC, it is clear that humans were cultivating grains by 200,000 years ago, as grain grinding stones have been found dating back to that time in Africa.[251] If millet was harvested in Eurasia prior to the onset of the Penultimate Glaciation, the crops would have failed drastically at the beginning of the glacial period, as millet is frost-sensitive and grows in soil that is 14 °C or warmer. Millet is a highly drought-resistant crop and therefore would have been one of the few crops that could have been grown in warmer climates during the arid glacial periods.

The names of the two kings Alulim and Alalngar translate as 'stag,' and 'pipe irrigator' respectively. These names are related to specific agricultural periods, stag implying animal husbandry, and pipe irrigator implying grain or vegetable cultivation. While there is no clear evidence of either animal husbandry or irrigated agriculture before the onset of the Penultimate Glaciation, there are the Dali-Man remains that were found along with ox remains dating back to 260,000 years ago.[252] The time-period of the Dali-Man remains correspond with the time-period of

---

plants in the Old World, third edition, Page 83

[251] R. Fullagar (2006) "Starch grains, stone tools and modern hominin behaviour." *An Archaeological Life: Papers in Honour of Jay Hall (Aboriginal and Torres Strait Islander Studies Unit Research Report Series 7)*. Pages 191-202

[252] J. L. Xiao, et al. (2002) "Age of the Fossil Dali Man in North-Central China deduced from Chronostratigraphy of the Loess-paleosol Sequence," *Quaternary Science Reviews*. 21 (20): 2191-2198

Alulim recorded in the Sumerian King Lists, between 266,379 and 237,579 BC. The Dali-Man remains were found in Dali County, Shaanxi Province, China, implying that the land of Eridu may have been in China. The remains of Dali-Man have been described as being either early homo-sapiens or late homo-erectus, implying that the first modern-humans may have originated in the region.

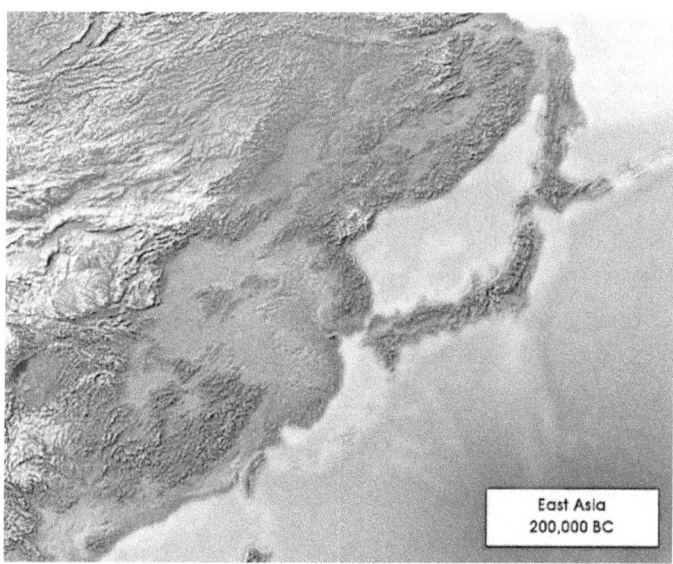

East Asia
200,000 BC

Conclusion

The current conventional Mesopotamian timeline of dynastic Mesopotamia is impossible. Believing in it means endorsing the idea the Egyptians lagged a thousand years behind the Sumerians technologically during the Middle Kingdom. This timeline forces the bronze age Harappan civilization to have existed as recently as 1200 BC, even as though iron age civilization had existed on the Ganges since at least 1800 BC. It is also not what the ancient Sumerians actually recorded, so believing it means believing that modern Assyriologists know more about ancient Sumer than the ancient Sumerians themselves. Given that the ancient Sumerians lived through it, and all Assyriologists have to go on is random bits of clay-tablets and mostly ruined city-mounds, this seems like an incredible stretch of the imagination. The fact is Assyriologists can't and don't need to explain the anachronisms, because the Mesopotamian timeline is synchronized with the Egyptian timeline, which Egyptologists insist on keeping as short as possible.

The idea that the ancient Sumerians built their earliest cities in the marshlands of Southern Iraq using stone imported from other countries is entirely illogical, they would have simply built them using mud-bricks as they did in the later periods. As the stone had to have been locally quarried, the region could not have been a marshland when the earliest cities were built, meaning that the oldest levels of Uruk and Eridu must date back to before the region began turning into a marshland circa 9,000 years ago. The fact that they switched to using mud-bricks simply proves that the water-levels rose during the course of Sumerian history, flooding their farmlands, and ultimately forcing the Mesopotamian cultures to migrate northward to Akkadia, Babylonia, and Assyria. The fact that Assyriologists ignore the ancient Sumerian records of the antediluvian era is probably for the best, as they cannot even accept that the 1st Kish Dynasty went back to 25,000 BC, even though it has been proven that grains were being farmed in the region at that time.

Unfortunately, the timeline of Egypt and Sumer are the two pillars that ancient history is built around. As the early Sumerians were trading with the early Egyptians, Assyriologists have been forced to synchronize the Mesopotamian timeline with the preposterous timeline used by Egyptologists. While this means that most of Sumerian history has to be ignored, it also affects the timelines of all other Eurasian cultures in contact with the Mesopotamians. The Harappan civilization of ancient India was trading with the Sumerians throughout its history and went into decline around the end of the Sumero-Akkadian dynastic period, which means the entire Harappan civilization is forced to correlate with the short Conventional Mesopotamian Timeline. This forces the entire Harappan timeline into a period of 2000 years, even though some of the archaeological sites in Pakistan and India have been carbon-dated back to over 8000 BC. These broken timelines then fan out further pulling the Minoans and Greeks, Iranians, and Chinese into this confusing mess.

Also Available

Broken Timelines – Book 1: Egypt

Broken Timelines – Book 2: Mesopotamia

Broken Timelines – Book 3: The Indo-Europeans and the Harappans